THE PIGORS INCIDENT PROCESS
OF CASE STUDY

The Instructional Design Library
Volume 29

THE PIGORS INCIDENT PROCESS OF CASE STUDY

Paul and Faith Pigors

Danny G. Langdon
Series Editor

**Educational Technology Publications
Englewood Cliffs, New Jersey 07632**

Library of Congress Cataloging in Publication Data

Pigors, Paul John William, 1900-
  The Pigors incident process of case study.

  (The Instructional design library; v. 29)
  Bibliography: p.
  1. Group work in education. 2. Teaching teams.
I. Pigors, Faith Cabot, 1904- joint author.
II. Title. III. Series: Instructional design
library; v. 29.
LB1032.P53   371.1'48   79-23530
ISBN 0-87778-149-4

Copyright © 1980 Educational Technology Publications, Inc., Englewood Cliffs, New Jersey 07632.

All rights reserved. No part of this book may be reproduced or transmitted, in any form or by any means, electronic or mechanical, including photocopying, recording, or by any information storage and retrieval system, without permission in writing from the Publisher.

Printed in the United States of America.

Library of Congress Catalog Card Number: 79-23530.

International Standard Book Number: 0-87778-149-4.

First Printing: March, 1980.

FOREWORD

There are few instructional designs that entirely meet the need to foster analytical problem-solving. It is even more difficult to find effective instructional guides for analyzing real-life situations—especially when, as so often occurs, time constraints for using them are rigid. The Pigors Incident Process (PIP) seems to offer solutions to these needs.

One of the things that has impressed me about PIP is that each part is simply described and easy to understand—yet, when all the aspects of PIP are put together, the result is an intricate piece of design work. As you read this book, you will readily grasp the "five-step cycle of case analysis." In the following chapters, you will also be provided with an in-depth description of a course structure and content which will enable you to use the analytical cycle for far more than academic problem-solving. The reader will also appreciate the many insights drawn by the authors from their years of experience. The final chapter, giving aids for implementation, makes the text still more practical.

Finally, without undervaluing other authors with whom I have had the pleasure of working on *The Instructional Design Library* series, I should like to add an expression of deep pleasure in having been briefly associated with two outstanding individuals—Paul and Faith Pigors. Their desire to do the best possible job of writing has made it a deeply satisfying experience for this editor.

Danny G. Langdon
Series Editor

PREFACE

This variant of orthodox case method was first developed and used (by the senior author, at the Massachusetts Institute of Technology) in 1950. It has been evolving ever since, chiefly owing to what we have learned from students of various ages and from different countries. But from the very beginning, the Pigors Incident Process (PIP, for short) has been an *experiential* form of case study. For this reason, it has proved effective in helping students to learn more—by analyzing cases—than is possible when case method consists merely in thinking and talking about what *other* people have said and done at other times and places.

One of the authors' basic tenets is that case method can be little more than an academic exercise *unless* those who engage in it become interested and able to apply, both during class hours and in daily living, ideas and attitudes which they recommend for "people in cases."

To implement this objective, PIP is designed to help students shift their focus, periodically, from *"those cases"* (the reported situations in which other people were participants) to *"this case"* (the ongoing situation of the study group itself), and then to *"everyday cases"* (situations outside of class in which members of the study group are responsible for making decisions and taking action in their daily lives).

Chapter I outlines a range of uses (applications) in a variety of learning-teaching situations.

Chapter II describes: (1) the five-step cycle of case analysis which characterizes PIP, and (2) the recommended structure for a full-length course in which *each cycle of case analysis merges with a continuing process of learning-teaching.* During the latter, teachers and students work toward shared objectives, and also share responsibility for results. A system of job rotation stimulates early volunteering by students, who form teaching teams, each responsible for one meeting. In every team, one member leads a case discussion. The other members render a written report containing observations on and evaluation of group performance (at the same meeting).

Chapter III provides a design format of: (1) PIP's analytical cycle, and (2) the recommended six-segment structure for a full-length PIP course. This section, therefore, shows what teachers and students actually do, as they interact during a progressive series of case discussions.

Chapter IV indicates desirable results ("OUTCOMES") which have repeatedly been achieved by this design for learning by *independent and responsible thinking, in cooperation with other group members.*

Chapter V gives a few reading references. Most of these contain case material already prepared, or readily convertible, for use by PIP.

The Appendix contains sample materials whose use helps to ensure that the desirable results listed can actually be achieved.

A brief preview of what is in this book would be incomplete without an expression of warmest gratitude to Danny G. Langdon. He urged us to write it, and then helped us to put it together. No author could ever wish for an editor who consistently responded with more promptness, patience, resilience, stick-to-it-iveness, and tact.

So, from the bottom of our hearts, "THANKS, Danny."

Paul and Faith Pigors

CONTENTS

FOREWORD v

PREFACE vii

ABSTRACT xi

   I. USE 3

  II. OPERATIONAL DESCRIPTION 9

 III. DESIGN FORMAT 23

 IV. OUTCOMES 77

   V. RESOURCES 91

 VI. APPENDIX 93

ABSTRACT

THE PIGORS INCIDENT PROCESS OF CASE STUDY

PIP is *an experiential form of case analysis.* Designed for group work, the first few case discussions are led by a teacher (or teaching team). But soon, students are encouraged to accept delegated responsibility for teaching (in volunteer teams). Each such team is responsible for one meeting: preparing case material, making a Discussion Plan, leading the group through a five-step cycle of case analysis, and afterwards writing a report which pictures group performance at that meeting.

This system of job rotation, along with judicious use of group dynamics, transforms orthodox case study from an academic exercise into a living experience of interaction. Case students can then see that *they are actually experimenting with what they are talking about.*

Formal tests play no part in this design. Instead, (1) early discussion of goals for the course encourages shared objectives, and (2) preparation (by outstanding students) of original cases, Discussion Plans, and performance reports, show what these leaders have learned. And cumulative case reporting builds a record of student perceptions as to what their associates have learned.

In these ways, self-validation of learning is built into this design, and usually each class becomes progressively involved in group appraisal of group performance.

Moreover, because, in PIP, each case that is analyzed consists of actual events, this design has a practical appeal, not only to college students, but also to adult study groups, especially in business and industry or in any other organization where management development is a major objective.

Because this instructional design is described operationally, as well as in general terms, it can be, and often has been, effectively used by instructors with no formal background in teaching.

THE PIGORS INCIDENT PROCESS
OF CASE STUDY

I.

USE

The Pigors Incident Process (PIP, for short) has multiple uses. Specific applications depend upon what this variant of the traditional case method is being *used for* (what learning ends are sought?); *with whom* it is used; and for *how long*. The effects of such determining factors can be glimpsed in the following list. But before enumerating a range of uses, two points should be emphasized: (1) wherever and however PIP is used, its *experiential* aspect elicits active and widespread participation, and (2) every case that is offered should be taken from a real-life situation. Both these PIP features ensure that course members can acquire practical know-how while also increasing their skills in productive interaction. PIP participants *learn by doing,* while listening to and talking with one another, and by *thinking*—both independently and cooperatively. They don't just sit back, more or less passively, in front of an instructor who does most of the talking. Specifically, what are some of the learning ends for which PIP has been used?

A Range of Uses

1. *In a single session* (two or three hours, with any number of participants up to 200 or so). For example, PIP has been used in this way by the American Management Association, and in various regional groups, *merely to demonstrate* its

3

characteristic five-step method of case analysis, and to give conferees one experience of how to work on a real-life situation in this way.

2. *In a PIP conference.* This may consist of three to six meetings, compressed into two or three days. Evidence that participants have benefited from a PIP conference has often been seen by the afternoon of the second day. At that point, a conferee may volunteer to present a first-hand experience— as a case for group analysis. Also, if the conference can be residential, perhaps over a weekend, learning-teaching is virtually certain to be carried on informally among conferees—during free time. However, a serious limitation inherent in holding PIP sessions so close together is that participants have little time, between meetings, to assimilate new ideas and to reflect on new experiences. Naturally, far more experience can be gained and shared—

3. *In a full-length course.* For in-house (or in-plant) purposes, such a course should consist of ten to 12 meetings, held at weekly intervals. A school semester offers far greater scope for making experiments and assimilating experiences. Anticipated results, therefore, may be commensurately greater.

4. *In a continuing and methodical process of self-development.* Many outstanding individuals have undertaken such a voluntary extension of PIP. Even during a brief conference, they have started to adopt this method as a habitual approach to current events and have begun to apply it as a way to learn and teach from what one lives through. It has often happened that conferees have recognized that the *five-step cycle* (or process) of case analysis can be incorporated into a larger and longer *process of learning-teaching,* when it is enhanced by other features of PIP. And the process of learning that starts during a conference (or full-length course) can be extended indefinitely. During such an inner-directed program for self-development, learning with and from other

people can be an integral part.

5. *In issue-oriented church or civic discussion groups.* PIP's analytical cycle, enhanced by its built-in small-group work, has occasionally and productively been used to: clarify individual thinking; step up objectivity; ensure orderly discussion; and prevent emotions from turning a discussion meeting into a bull session or an acrimonious, partisan confrontation. Judging from limited experience, this use could profitably be applied by church or civic groups to controversial and divisive issues, such as racial discrimination (including reverse discrimination and quotas); locating and building nuclear reactors; developing the neutron bomb; and establishing (or reestablishing) diplomatic relations between the U.S.A. and countries with whom we have serious disagreements. This list of topics could be lengthened indefinitely. PIP could well be applied even at the high-school level, in courses on history and current events.

6. *By committees of scientists.* Because PIP is a problem-solving technique and is designed to stimulate cooperative thinking among members of small groups, it could well be used by task forces to solve scientific problems. PIP's special contributions might be: (a) bringing all relevant information before the problem-solving group so that everyone can look at it together; (b) clarifying the reasons for differences of opinion; and (c) helping decision-makers to *integrate differences* by agreeing on what seem to be the most compelling reasons to support a preferred solution.

7. *In developing countries.* It has been taken for granted that literacy is a prerequisite for case analysis. But modern achievements in audio-visual aids may have made that assumption obsolete. For example, if every PIP Incident were filmed, non-literate people could use PIP in small groups to clarify their thinking on divisive issues, such as planned parenthood, and equal opportunities for girls and women in education and paid employment.

While touching on a variety of *learning ends* that can be attained by using PIP, we have necessarily brought in the question of *learning environments*. These two aspects of a learning-teaching process cannot realistically be regarded as though they were entirely separate. But, certainly, they are not identical. Let's now shift our primary focus to—

Learning Environments

Since 1950, many thousands of people have used PIP in colleges; business and industrial organizations (not only in the U.S.A., but also overseas, and in national cultures as different from ours as those of Mexico, India, and Japan); in hospitals; government agencies; and in all branches of the U.S. military service. Up to now, PIP has always been used at the level of adult education—in graduate courses or as continuing education after employment.

An Overall Aim and Sub-goals

For most PIP users, in business and industry, for example, the long-term aim has been to help people develop their full managerial and executive potential. To the extent that all steps in PIP's analytical cycle become *mental habits,* case students attain the following sub-goals in progressing toward the long-term aim:

In Step 1: Paying close attention to a small incident. A question to be considered in Step 1 is: Might this superficially trivial event be a significant signal that something is going seriously wrong?

In Step 2: Getting and organizing facts. (a) Gaining skill in asking information-seeking questions, to 'get around' in an ongoing situation, without overlooking any potentially significant aspect. (b) Becoming increasingly efficient in organizing factual information, by omitting relatively insignificant items and condensing essentials into a concise yet comprehensive and objectively worded summary.

In Step 3: Seeking relationships and formulating a short-term issue. (a) Learning to view key elements (facts) in the perspective of a larger context, (the case as a whole), regarding them as interactive factors (forces). (b) *Mastering the technique of determining what is at stake,* 'here and now' (at the time of a troublesome incident), and phrasing that opinion as a *short-term action issue* (a question to be answered in prompt decision).

In Step 4: Decision-making. Improving one's capabilities to: (a) Choose among various options for short-term action. (b) Interact productively with other people (by listening as well as talking) in a small group, to clarify, appraise, and consolidate *different reasons,* all of which are intended to support the *same decision.* (c) Effectively present a subgroup opinion (perhaps including some degree of dissent). (d) Compare different decisions, to appraise them. Which decision seems most likely to stand up: because it is valid in principle; takes account of costs, human as well as financial; and meets the test of common sense?

In Step 5: Learning to think at the level of policy. Acquiring the knack of *three-dimensional vision* to reflect on a situation, after having made a decision for short-term action. What further action, if any, seems called for after: (a) *looking back* over the whole sequence of events and behavior; (b) *looking forward* toward long-term, organization-wide goals; (c) *looking upward* to the level of policy?

Having now introduced PIP, in a general way, by listing various uses, learning environments, and goals, it is time to get down to cases—with an *operational description.*

II.

OPERATIONAL DESCRIPTION

A. Using PIP's Analytical Cycle

However long the period during which PIP is used (a single session, a conference, or a full-length course), a basic feature that is always applied is a five-step cycle of case analysis.

Induction into this work method may take one of two forms:
- receiving, in advance, a written outline of the five-step cycle; or
- at the start of the meeting when the first case is to be analyzed, the person in charge (a teacher or training director) may provide a brief oral explanation (clarified by a visual display of the five steps on tear-sheets, chalkboard, or overhead transparency). In this way, students are shown, as well as told, what will be expected of them—*technically*.

Before describing what students will be doing in applying PIP's analytical cycle, it may be well to mention *two things that they won't need to do:*

1. *They won't be expected to listen to a lecture* which expounds the nature of PIP. The best way to get acquainted with PIP is to practice it. What PIP is, and what it might do—for students who use it for all it is worth—will become apparent as it is applied.

2. *They won't have to read a lengthy case report* (as is

required in traditional case method), before setting to work on a case. In fact, *they won't be required to read any case report,* at any stage of the course.

And now for *what students will be doing* as they systematically apply PIP's analytical cycle to:
- pay close attention to a small-scale incident;
- ferret out surrounding facts in a total case situation;
- consider what is at stake 'here and now'—at the time of the incident;
- determine what decisions and actions would need to be taken by *insiders in that case* to cope with the incident; and
- reflect upon needs for long-term action, extracting a full measure of meaning from each case discussed in the study group.

To analyze a case by PIP is to explore a given territory. The task is that of a hunter. In that role, students will be searching not only for objectively verifiable data, but also for facts-of-feeling and for a variety of implicit meanings. Every step in this quest for information and meaning will be characterized by a general question. Each such question needs to be answered before taking the next step.

STEP 1: Starting with an Incident.

Students set out on their analytical journey by diving straight into the middle of the action. They are invited to imagine that this troublesome Incident has just occurred. A study group may first see an Incident on film. Or, it may be role-played for them. But, in any event, they will always receive a written script (half a page or so in length). Appended to that document will be a "Suggestion for Getting into the Case." By accepting that suggestion to "come on in and help to cope with an incident," students find that they feel responsible for taking decisive action. The Incident becomes *their* problem. Along with the Incident and its appended suggestion, students also receive a partial organization chart. A glance at this chart tells them *who* and *where* they are, *organizationally* – in the suggested (collective) role of an insider who has to cope with the Incident.

At this first step, the characteristic question (to be answered by each course member *independently*) is: *What clues can I find that need to be followed up* by getting relevant information before even attempting to determine what is immediately at stake in the case, still less deciding what should be done about it? As individual students put that question to themselves, they will be testing their capabilities:

- to read between the lines as well as along them; and
- to glimpse underlying issues and inner motivating forces that affect outward behavior. How did this incident look, and what did it feel like, to the people who were caught up in that climactic event? Did someone see it as a significant straw in the wind? To another insider did it look like the "last straw"?

While studying an Incident, students may wish to make marginal notes, (indicating possible leads), or to underline a few words which seem especially significant. As soon as everyone in the group has taken Step 1, it will be time to start peppering the discussion leader with information-seeking questions.

Here is a sample Incident along with a "Suggestion for Getting into the Case."

SAMPLE INCIDENT: Ms. Hillory's Ultimatum

> As the scene opens, Juanita Hillory (a senior employee in the Travel Section), is just entering the office of David Brown (newly appointed Section Supervisor). Brown has been greatly pleased at the many congratulations he has received during the week that he has been in this position.
>
> BROWN (smiling, and indicating a chair): Won't you sit down,

> Ms. Hillory? I'm glad you asked for this appointment. I've been wanting a chance to talk with you.
> HILLORY (brusquely): No, I prefer to speak my piece standing up. Did you know that just before Mr. Russell left, he promised me the job of assistant supervisor?
> BROWN (obviously taken aback): No, I . . .
> HILLORY (interrupting): Well, he did, and I just want to tell you that I'm not going to be sweet-talked out of this. I want to know *what you're going to do about it.*
> BROWN (in a puzzled, but friendly, tone): Do sit down, Ms. Hillory, so we . . .
> HILLORY (angrily): No, I will *not* sit down. And I won't stand still, either, for another run-around. I'll give you one week to make up your mind. Then, if I have to, I'll go higher up.
> On the heels of this challenge, Ms. Hillory storms out of the office. Brown immediately picks up the phone and calls his predecessor.
> BROWN: Say, Russell, did you tell Hillory you'd recommend her for the position of assistant supervisor? . . . You did? Wow! That really puts me on the spot.

Suggestion for Getting into the Case

Try to imagine yourself in the position of David Brown, newly appointed supervisor of the Travel Section. In view of key facts (when you get them) and of what seems to be at stake here, how might you handle this *Incident*? And, what further action, if any, might you take in the *ongoing case situation*?

(We're not suggesting that you try to second-guess what Brown actually did. It will be more useful for you to imagine that you are in his organizational role at the time of this Incident. His difficulties and opportunities are yours. Use your best judgment, as a responsible management representative.)

STEP 2: Finding and Summarizing Facts on the Whole Case (to the End of the Incident).

Any such script (if reasonably well-written) can be counted on to trigger widespread participation in fact-finding. Sometimes, aggressive course members pop up with so many questions that the pressure to recognize everyone precipitates a mini-incident for the discussion leader. Judg-

Operational Description

ment and tact are needed to ensure equal opportunity for all would-be questioners, while keeping Step 2 within due time limits. (Recommendations for achieving both objectives are given in the "Design Format" chapter.) During the first exercise of case analysis by PIP, fact-finding will probably have to be limited to a mere sampling.

In most groups, Step 2 is relatively inefficient the first time it is attempted. But, with practice, two time-saving devices can become habitual: (1) using a systematic search pattern, and (2) developing cooperative questioning. (These techniques are described in Chapter III and the Appendix.) Few PIP participants start with the insight that haphazard questioning is inefficient. Therefore, results of the many questions asked about the first case are likely to be inadequate in two ways:

- coverage of the case as a whole is virtually certain to be incomplete; and
- the information that has been obtained is a welter of apparently unrelated items.

For effective use in decision-making, an unorganized mass of factual material needs first to be reduced to manageable proportions (by throwing out relatively insignificant items), and then to be put in order (both logically and chronologically). Here's where the valuable skill of summarizing comes into play. As at any effectively conducted committee meeting, the makings of a decision come into sharp focus as soon as someone states concisely the essence of what has been said.

However, a difficulty which often crops up in case analysis, when it's time for a summary, is that some people see this as an opportunity to state opinions. A classic example of that view was given by a course member who started his summary like this: "Well, we all know the guy is guilty." But according to PIP standards, an appropriate summary omits all judgments and is confined to statements of verified facts. Key facts of the case are grouped into coherent blocks—beginning with information about the earliest events in the case situation and ending with a digest of the Incident, which is where the study group is 'now.'

PIP is a naturally *selective mechanism*, in various ways. Therefore, two things are predictable about this second part of Step 2: (1) If the first summarizer is a volunteer, that individual will probably be among the more aggressive members in the study group. (2) A person who makes an effective summary will be an outstanding member and one of the natural leaders.

If there are serious gaps in an off-the-cuff summary, these can be filled in by a written summary (prepared in advance for distribution at this time). In any event, the paragraphing of a written summary can be helpful as a link to the next phase, where analytical thinking moves to center stage.

STEP 3: Seeing Key Facts as Interrelated Factors and Agreeing on an Action Issue.

The above heading indicates the two-part question which characterizes this crucial stage of case analysis: (1) Looking at the now unified blocks of information, what significant interrelationships can be seen? (2) What statement of the short-term action issue is acceptable to the study group? 'Everyone knows' that the way in which a question for decision is formulated goes far to determine the answer that will be given. Therefore, in PIP, we emphasize the need to think carefully about the question (or issue) that is to be decided, instead of jumping straight from facts to decisions.

Perhaps the first suggestion (offered by a course member) as to the immediate issue will bring disagreement from some other participant. So much the better, if the final formulation combines the best thinking that can be developed in the group-at-large. For example, in regard to the Hillory Incident, simplistic issue formulations that have been suggested include: "Shall I, in Brown's position, give in to Hillory? Or shall I tell her where she gets off? Or, would it be smarter to buck the decision upstairs?" Answering any such oversimplified questions wouldn't get anyone far toward reaching the goal of developing managerial potential. For that purpose, a more open-ended question is useful. For instance, "Confronted with such an Incident, how might I (in Brown's position, and at this stage in my career) best promote the goals of the Travel Section and of the Agency as a whole?" Having agreed on some such issue, productive and orderly discussion during the next step becomes possible.

STEP 4: Decisions and Reasoning.

During this phase, a three-fold question is first tackled in subcommittees: (1) "What is the best opinion (decision and reasoning) that our subgroup can work out for coping with the Incident? (2) How can we show that 'our' option for decision is preferable to any of the others? (3) How can we *most effectively present* our opinion to the group-at-large?"

Here is a list of the suboperations during which the Step 4 question is answered. (The "Design Format" chapter supplies more details.)

a. From a range of options (displayed by a leader), course members make individual choices.

b. Like-minded members (who have selected the same option) then meet together in subcommittees to sort out and consolidate their reasoning.

c. Next, the various subcommittee decisions are presented to the group-at-large, by spokespersons or role-players, or in both ways.

d. Time permitting, the various decisions and presentations are compared and appraised by the whole study group.

With or without suboperation *d,* when time runs out for Step 4, course members will have done a lot of hard work on a case. And, perhaps, they will feel they have finished with it.

Having decided how to handle an immediate difficulty, do we need to do anything more? In the authors' opinion, what still needs to be done is to take the most practical step of all.

STEP 5: Reflecting on Major Issues and Long-Term Organization-wide Goals.

At this stage of the PIP game, the *general* question is: If we now *review* the whole case (up to the end of the Incident), what ideas can we see which seem practical for us to experiment with in our regular work (and life) situations? Here's where PIP can help case students to gain and share more experience than most people find time to winnow out from the bounteous crop of events that constantly pours out before them. And a great advantage for members of a study group is that they can practice the skill of generalizing from experience. In this way, case students can derive a special kind of experiential insight which everyone needs every day. Many busy managers and supervisors seem to feel that having dealt with an incident, they can't afford to spend any more time on it. Perhaps some other incident is already staring them in the face and must be coped with 'right now.' In this respect, members of a case study group have the edge on many of their organizational colleagues. PIP practitioners *do* have time for reflection. They can also benefit from 'leading' questions as they make a new beginning in their continuing quest for meaning.

At the start of Step 5, the study group again divides into subcommittees. The composition of each subgroup is (usually) determined by individual selection among three broad-gauged questions about the case situation as a whole. The specific questions used by the Pigors team are given in the "Design Format" chapter. Taken together, they invite attention to:

- *what seems to have been accountable* (not who was

Operational Description

to blame) *for what went wrong* (negative factors in the case situation);
- *what favorable (positive) factors* were, or might have been, used as resources; and
- *what opportunities for long-term action* might implement corporate policies while moving toward organization-wide goals.

If the time schedule permits, the three columns of answers reported by subcommittee spokespersons (and displayed by the discussion leader where everyone can see them), can be correlated and compared. Several minutes should be reserved to look beyond the confines of the case-for-the-day. Which factors (positive or negative) and which long-term goals can be seen as *common denominators* between that case and other situations where people depend upon one another for results? And which of these common denominators might usefully be acted upon in the daily work (and life) situations where members of this study group take action and make decisions?

The Analytical Cycle as Part of a Process

Deriving full benefit from all the opportunities offered during PIP's steps of case analysis is in itself a process; and it is a tall order. But experience (during almost 30 years) has shown that college students and management representatives can measure up to it. To help them do so, the authors recommend that a full-length course be structured as a series in which participants can make progress during *six distinct, but related, segments,* as described in the following section of this chapter.

B. A Progressive Series of Meetings
SEGMENT 1: The Mutual Orientation Meeting.
This meeting consists of: (a) mutual introductions; (b) the

beginning of orientation; and (c) initial induction into techniques of the work method. Productive introductions to fellow students (or other co-workers) require more than merely sharing information as to names and organizational positions. *Mutual acquaintance* can begin when individual course members indicate *who* each one of them is, by expressing some of their assumptions, attitudes, value judgments, and current degree of sensitivity and perceptivity.

Also at the first meeting, the process of getting acquainted can merge with the beginnings of teamwork. This fusion comes about when conferees discuss goals to shoot for during the course as a whole. (At the appropriate time, a draft copy—prepared by the leader—can be distributed, as a basis for discussion.) Such target-setting enables participants to compare their current individual goals with those proposed for them during the course. To the extent that the two sets of objectives can be harmonized, shared purpose becomes a reality beginning at the first meeting.

Toward the close of a first session, *technical induction* can start as the leader briefly explains the five-step cycle which course members will first use at the next meeting, the start of—

SEGMENT 2: Demonstration and Practice Sessions.

During this part of a PIP course, standards of technical performance in case analysis can be established and progressively raised. There are two or three sessions, according to the length of the course and the judgment of the leader. The pace of increasing proficiency can be accelerated if, after each practice session, course members receive a written report on group performance. Each such report should contain a selection of facts-as-perceived by the official observer, supplemented by a few evaluative comments, and questions or recommendations regarding possible changes in performance.

Long experience shows that progress by case students

toward the goal of managerial development depends, in part, on the availability of a continuing record of group performance. This record consists of a series of written reports, rendered to the group after each case discussion. Observations and notes for these reports are made by the staff member on each leading team, who functions as an *official observer-reporter.* For the "first team," there are obvious advantages in having the same partners work together throughout a full-length course or, better still, for many courses. Aside from specific duties performed by these partners, before, during, and after each meeting, members of the "first team" serve as role models for student teams that volunteer to lead group discussion later in the course.

After the practice sessions, progress toward the goal of management development can be made at a special kind of meeting—one that resembles an interim summary of *"This Case"* (the ongoing situation of the study group itself).

SEGMENT 3: An Interim "Progress Review."

This meeting helps students to shift the center of their attention from "historical case situations" to what has been happening around the conference table. Using essentially the same analytical method which they have been applying to "those cases" presented as starters, conferees begin their progress review by working in small groups. The facts and ideas on which they now focus are drawn from their own memories of preceding meetings, as well as from the written reports. The assignment to be met now is to determine:
- What has gone well in our work together so far, and why?
- Might we make even more progress, by changing any of our ways of thinking, talking, listening, and otherwise interacting, in the meetings that are coming up?
- Which of various suggestions for making changes shall we decide—by consensus—to implement?

Taking stock and making plans, in this way, leads PIP participants to the brink of the Great Divide. When they cross it, they will open up new territory as volunteer teams, each of which: prepares a case of its own, leads discussion on it, and writes a report of group performance that day. Usually, at least two volunteer teams have already signed up by the fourth or fifth meeting of a study group. Another team, perhaps two, may volunteer at the end of the first stock-taking meeting. But because supervisors, managers, and staff specialists are busy people, PIP now includes an extra session. This special kind of meeting constitutes the fourth part of a full-length course.

SEGMENT 4: The Working Session.

This meeting enables volunteer teams to start (or continue) preparing cases for group discussion. Such preparation includes writing (or editing) an Incident, and planning for group work during all five phases of PIP's analytical cycle. To complete their preparatory work, most teams hold another working session outside of scheduled course hours.

Next comes the fifth part of a progressive series, consisting of three or four meetings, sometimes referred to as—

SEGMENT 5: "Highlights of the Week."

They certainly look like highlights to the volunteer teams that have undertaken to be responsible for them. During these sessions, the "first team" takes the seats vacated by the leaders-for-the-day, and engages in the same tasks (though with certain self-imposed restrictions) that are always performed by regular members of a study group. (The "Design Format" chapter will amplify the preceding sentence by describing the multiple roles played by a "first team" throughout a course, regardless of who is undertaking specific delegated responsibilities for planning and conducting a given session. The Appendix includes material for use by volunteers

Operational Description

who are (a) preparing a case and planning for group discussion, and (b) functioning in the role of an official observer-reporter.)

A full-length PIP course is rounded off by —

SEGMENT 6: A Final Stock-taking and Planning Session.

Now, group members can 'put it all together.' Starting in small groups, they confer about, and later report on:
- benefits which they—as volunteer discussion leaders and observer-reporters, respectively—derived from the extra work they put in, as well as:
- their perceptions and appraisals of group performance—both technical and human—throughout the course. In doing this evaluating, *primary emphasis is on changes made since the mid-course review meeting.*

Usually, all three subcommittees (leaders, observer-reporters, and performance appraisers) come up with ideas for making minor modifications during future PIP courses. If time permits, the group-at-large may also offer suggestions to be displayed on a *composite diagram of major issues.* Such a diagram shows needs for long-term action that stand out in connection with several—or all—of the cases discussed, including "This Case." (Communicating and Style of Managing have always been among the issues displayed on this diagram—a sample of which is given in the Appendix.)

To an experienced teacher, perhaps everything described in this chapter sounds "as easy as falling off a log." But is it? Many years of learning-teaching by PIP have shown that leading such a progressive series of meetings is neither easy nor impossible. The next chapter contains a number of how-to-do-it suggestions for teachers and students.

III.
DESIGN FORMAT

This chapter is structured in the same general way as the "Operational Description" chapter; that is, beginning with the five-step cycle of case analysis and then taking up the design of a progressive series of meetings. But now we'll flesh out the barebones description of PIP's 'what' and 'how,' giving illustrative material to show what students and teachers do, as they move through the analytical steps, and how PIP participants can be helped progressively to raise standards of their technical performance as well as the quality of their social interaction.

A. Applying the Five-Step Cycle

There are two significant differences between the Incident that we use this time and the one given in the preceding chapter. One difference is in the context of this Incident—which is part of a situation that arose in an insurance company. The second difference consists in the approach that we invite from readers. As you study the following Incident, can you imagine: (1) that you are a member of a PIP study group (either a college student or a management representative—line or staff); and (2) that this Incident will launch you on your first exercise in case analysis? (If you actually *were* such a student, enrolled in a full-length course, you would be presented with your first case at the second meeting. Probably all you would know about the analytical cycle would be an outline of the five steps, including lists of the various suboperations which belong in each phase.) Here, then, is a sample Incident.

Case Title: "Staff/Line Communication Blocks"
Incident: Betty Is Bounced Back

> George Bombara (Manager, General Agency Contracts Division) is in his semi-enclosed private office. John Baker, Assistant Manager, is working at his desk just outside Bombara's office.
> BOMBARA: John, could I see you a minute?
> BAKER (getting up): Sure, right away (seating himself near the manager's desk). What's new?
> BOMBARA (his voice quivering with indignation): This really is *too* bad! I just had a call from Mr. March, requesting an *immediate* replacement for Miss Brown. March said, "That girl is impossible! Her work is all wrong. She can't do *anything* right..."
> BAKER: I'm very much surprised. Surely Betty is one of our most accurate girls. In fact, wasn't that one reason why we decided she was the best qualified clerk to be trained for promotion to Section B?
> BOMBARA: It certainly was. That's what gets me. But do you remember how reluctant she was to accept that temporary reassignment to the Special Project Unit? It seems to me Miss Brown has deliberately been doing poor work there, so they'd send her back to us. We certainly can't let her force our hand like that.
> BAKER: I entirely agree, Sir. We can't tolerate that kind of behavior.
> BOMBARA: Right! Well, you take care of it.

Suggestion for Getting into the Case

Try to imagine yourself in Mr. Baker's position as Assistant Manager.

In view of the facts (when you get them) and of what seems to be at stake here, how might you handle *this Incident?* What further action, if any, might you take *in the ongoing case situation?*

(We're not suggesting that you attempt to take on Mr. Baker's personality, but merely that you imagine yourself as being in his organizational role at the time of this Incident. And, in asking what you might do, we mean *at best.* Using your best judgment, what course of action do you think you could look back on without wishing you had done something different?)

See Figure 1 for an organization chart given to students studying this case. The importance of the chart will become clear as we proceed through this chapter.

Administrative Responsibilities During Step 1.

It might seem that leaders would have nothing to do in Step 1. But actually their role includes obligations even during periods when—at least in theory—no one says anything. In fact, a major responsibility for the discussion leader, in Step 1, is seeing to it that *no one does say anything* until the slower (or more thorough) thinkers have finished studying the brief script. At that point (if this is a first exercise in applying the PIP cycle), there's another responsibility to be met: This is to emphasize the implications of the "Suggestion" which is appended to the Incident. Experience has repeatedly shown that case students often skip this part of the assignment. However, unless they understand and accept the invitation to work on the case *in the collective role of a responsible insider,* conferees are likely to start riding off in all directions instead of forming an organized search party. In this respect, PIP is highly directive.

During these first few minutes (in Step 1), even when no one is speaking, a leader's teammate (the official observer-reporter) also has responsibilities. Individual differences among course members can be noted. These differences may prove significant, both later in the first session and as the course progresses. Who shows what signs of setting to work promptly and seriously on the Incident? Who, if anyone, merely reads it through rapidly and, casting a quick glance at

26   *The Pigors Incident Process of Case Study*

Figure 1

CASE: "Staff/Line Communication Blocks"
Partial Organization Chart — Agency Contracts Department

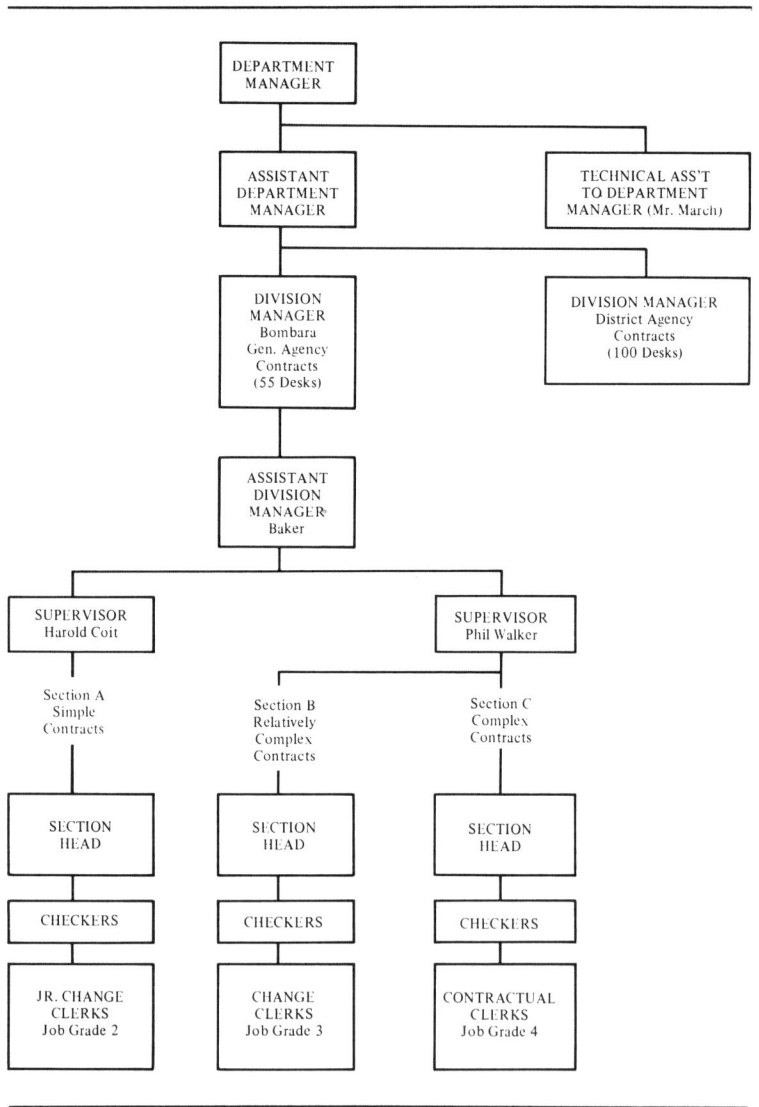

Design Format

the corporate organization chart accompanying the Incident, begins to doodle, to look around the room, or even (unless restrained by the discussion leader), chats with a neighbor? Notes taken now, on observable signs of inner motivation, can be used as case material later. Were these early indications of a lackadaisical attitude which persists? If so, how will other course members respond to that attitude? What changes, if any, can be observed later in the behavior of someone who seemed 'turned off' by the first Incident?

Leadership Responsibilities in Connection with Step 2.

Possibilities for helping course members do their best in Step 2 can conveniently be subdivided according to the time factor. They can be capitalized on *before, during,* and *after* this second phase of case analysis. Usually, these preliminaries are relevant only when PIP participants are analyzing their first case.

BEFORE: According to recent PIP practice, a sample case summary is distributed to course members about a week before they tackle their first case. This summary relates to a case that will *not* be discussed by members of the study group during this course. Experience has shown that advance study of such a sample summary can be productive; but also that in many study groups, some members barely glance at it. This lack of interest (and of foresight) may later prove to have been a handicap. But when the time comes for participants to assemble information on the case-for-the-day, there are other ways in which a discussion leader can help case students take an interest in the task at hand, and to accept the necessary time constraint. Here are two such ways: (1) Just before information-seeking starts, on the first case to be analyzed, a leader may wish to point out that the task coming up is probably familiar to all (or most) of those present. When supervisors or managers notice some troublesome incident, what action do they take next? *They get facts.* What they need is a whole range of objectively verifiable information to give them an all-around, solidly-based understanding of the situation in which the incident built up. This task is precisely what members of a study group will be performing in Step 2. It will be easier than it can be in most work situations because now they can get all the necessary information by questioning one person, the discussion leader. (2) A second helpful move by a discussion leader just before course members embark on Step 2 is to alert them to the probability that there won't be enough time to answer all the questions which they would like to ask. This constraint arises from the fact that inexperienced information seekers tend to get fact-happy. They are likely to go on asking questions long after that task has ceased to be productive. One reason for relatively low productivity, the first time around, is that each person's listening tends to be at a low level while *other people's questions* are being answered. The result is that repeat questions waste everyone's time. Moreover, a major objective, during every exercise in case analysis, is to complete essential tasks in all five analytical phases. By offering some such explanation before questioning starts, a discussion leader can indicate that the clock should be regarded as the boss factor—not only in Step 2, but also in succeeding phases. This explanation may alert some course members to the need for listening attentively to *all* information imparted by the discussion leader (whether or not it answers any questions of their own). By the second or third practice session, PIP participants may be able to complete their fact-finding in about 20 minutes (approximately the length of time which can reasonably be allotted to this task). In that event, there will be no need for a leader to shut off questioning. This desirable development can be anticipated if members of an alert group are guided by an experienced and tactful leader who observes certain do's and don'ts. To be specific:

Design Format

DURING Step 2, PIP leaders (course directors or volunteer leaders-for-the-day) should—

• Have in mind all essential information on the case (insofar as it is available). A single worksheet (prepared in advance) with key names and dates, can instantly clue a leader into any item which may not come immediately to mind—during haphazard questioning.

• Have at hand copies of any factual information which is easier to take in by eye than by ear (a ground plan, for example) or which needs to be studied with care and referred to at a later stage of case analysis (for example, some provision in an existing labor agreement, a company rule, or a statement of corporate policy).

• Keep answers brief, and word them objectively.

• Try, without squelching anybody, to offer equal opportunity to all would-be questioners. If a few aggressive course members continually speak up without waiting to be recognized, a leader can suggest that they postpone some of their questions until others have had a chance to speak.

• Encourage questioning that is efficient, because this enables information seekers to "get around" in a case situation, and to do so cooperatively. At first, there is likely to be little *follow-through* by any members of questions asked by someone else. By the second practice session, it is usually possible to interest at least some participants (especially those who have studied the Fact-Finding Table in the observer's written report) in the idea that time can be saved, and summarizing made easier, if they dig into one area of the case at a time, instead of making haphazard stabs at the job. This emerging appreciation as to the value of systematic fact-finding can be encouraged by a leader who suggests that: (1) anyone who wishes to follow through on a lead opened up by someone else may ask two (or even three) consecutive questions on that same topic (instead of being constrained by the customary one-at-a-time rule). Such follow-through may be interrupted only by another question along the same line. (2) This extra-question allowance may also be given to participants who wish to follow up a significant question of their own. (See Appendix for recommended search pattern.)

- Refrain from volunteering information which has not been specifically requested. But especially in a *first* fact-finding exercise, a supportive leader may decide to extend some answer by adding a bit of closely related information. Such an addition may be enough to start fact-finders off on a topic about which they haven't yet inquired. On the other hand, a hard-nosed leader may decide that it will be more educational, in the long run, for students to go ahead this time and make decisions without some of the information which they need. Leaders who take that position are saying, in effect, "The embarrassment which these students will feel when they find out later what they overlooked now, will teach them not to be so careless in the future." However, to adopt that view is to ignore or underestimate the demoralizing effect of being shown up as incompetent. A leader who recognizes the importance of high morale and mounting self-confidence, as factors in progress, will look for legitimate ways to help course members do an adequate job, even when analyzing their first case. A more subtle device than the slightly extended answer is to—

- Call for an interim summary. When a seriously incomplete set of facts is *assembled,* the resulting structure has obvious holes in it. Such gaps jump to the eye of an alert beholder, being recognized as openings for a more extended search. In other words, to see what you've got so far, as verified factual information, makes it easier to see what you still need to look for.

- Don't insist that course members adopt a systematic search pattern. If no one picks up the idea, a leader should drop it—at least for the present. Perhaps during the first 'progress review' meeting (later in the course), someone will suggest trying it out (especially if reports on group performance show that fact-finding is still inefficient and include a brief statement describing a search pattern).

- Don't give your opinion when answering questions (in Step 2). For example, a course member may ask: "Should Betty be disciplined, or demoted?" Confronted with such an *opinion-seeking question,* a leader may answer (in effect): "The opinions that will count most, for you, are yours—not mine. At present, our mutual task is to bring out the information that you need as a basis for informed opinions of your own."

- Don't invent 'facts' that aren't there. Why not? In the first place, a case that is even partly hypothetical is to that extent less useful, as a vehicle for decision-making, than a faithful reproduction of the 'real thing.' Second, from a discussion leader's point of view, to go in for invention, rather than sticking to straight reporting, is incompatible with the spirit of case method. Moreover, it doesn't even pay off—for the inventor—in the short run. Leaders who indulge in a bit of fictionalizing are almost certain to become entangled in the web they weave (especially since the weaving has to be done at a rapid pace with no time to make notes). When a leader is asked for information that isn't available, the sensible response is: "I'm sorry, but I haven't got that information." When working from an adequate case report, it is possible to add: "And we don't need that information at this point. In everyday life, all of us must often make decisions without *all* the information that we'd like to have. I suggest that we do that now."

- Don't present inferences under the guise of facts. Inferences can be useful. In some areas of certain cases, for instance concerning the 'Why' of someone's behavior, a reasonable inference may be as close to a fact as one can get. When offering an inference, in reply to a question about facts, a leader should: (1) frankly state that the answer has been *inferred* from facts, and (2) briefly supply the inductive reasoning.

- Don't just cut off information-seeking questions by curtly announcing: "Time's up." The following procedure works better. When the timespan allotted for fact-finding has elapsed, leaders who have previously alerted course members that 20 minutes is about as much time as can reasonably be spent on that task, can rely on the clock as well as on their own flexibility and tact. Even if questions are still coming thick and fast, a leader can point to the clock and say (in effect): "As you can see, it's about time now to wind up this part of our work. But we *could* take two or three more questions, if participants have a few which they urgently wish to ask." When final questions have been answered (and usually there would be more, if time permitted), a leader can help course members tackle the next task. If this is the first exercise in case analysis, a leader may wish to suggest that before anyone volunteers to sum up, everyone should take a brief look at the sample summary which was distributed in advance. Using the general form of that document as a guide, who will volunteer to do the *same kind of thing* with reference to the case-for-the-day?

Now comes what many people experience as the first difficult task in case analysis. How many course members can winnow facts as they come in, on the fly, during a rapid-fire question-and-answer period?

At the start of a PIP course, a leader is well advised to settle for an oral summary—from students—that is somewhat incomplete. At worst, no one volunteers, or can easily be persuaded to undertake the whole job alone. If that happens, summarizing can be made into a *group project.* It is usually easy to get a volunteer to make a start by offering a block of information about some key person or area of the case under

Design Format

discussion. And once a start has been made, other course members can be expected to contribute other blocks of information. However, even the product of group effort may contain serious gaps. Or, perhaps an inference was stated when a fact was available. Occasionally, a contrary-to-fact statement creeps in. Some of these flaws are likely to be spotted and corrected by other course members. Nevertheless, even with such on-the-spot editing, a first effort at summing up salient facts of a case is likely to be inadequate. Therefore, students may be invited briefly to study copies of a written summary of the case-for-the-day. This digest of facts will have been prepared in advance by the discussion leader. (Readers should not confuse this summary with the *sample summary*—of another case—distributed at the first meeting, to indicate the *general form* of a case summary.)

A well-written summary can be useful to case students in three ways. (1) Its paragraphing indicates how facts can be consolidated into blocks—regardless of the sequence in which they became available. (2) A written summary serves as a reminder of the gist of a case. And (3) its organization by paragraphs in a given sequence, suggests how (in Step 3) blocks of facts may be seen as interrelated parts of a whole.

Staff responsibilities during and after Step 2: The staff member on each leading team is responsible for rendering to group members—after each exercise in case analysis—a written report on group performance. To be fully useful, part of this report (based on notes taken during the question-and-answer period) should consist in a Fact-Finding Table, which (1) indicates the sequence and topic of each question, (2) identifies each questioner by number (in code or according to numbers on tent cards), and (3) is distributed to course members in time for careful study before the next meeting.

STEP 3: Helping Students to Visualize Interactive Factors and Agree on an Action Issue.

Having sorted out what group members see as the essentials of a case, PIP participants can take further measures to ensure that the decisions which they are about to make are likely to stand up, because they are not only based on a comprehensive view of verified facts, but also on the recognition that these facts are interactive. Whatever affects one factor will bring about some degree of change in all the others. The idea that key factors are interactive is easy to state. But it is not so easy to implement in a specific decision.

In a case study group, an effective way to illustrate this concept of interaction is to diagram key elements of a case—showing how they interlink. Figure 2 gives a sample, complete with a key which specifies sub-factors for each topical heading.

Making such a diagram (or merely listing interactive factors, if course members prefer) requires analytical skill of a relatively high order. Systems-minded course members (perhaps from an EDP department) can do it 'on their heads.' Often, some of them (having received a sample diagram in advance) have already done it, *in* their heads—or on a note pad—by the end of Step 2. But many other people enter a PIP course with little of this useful skill.

Because this kind of learning comes primarily by *doing,* it is undesirable to have any one person do the whole job for other group members. Probably the least useful practice (though tempting because it is the quickest) is to have the discussion leader present the group with a ready-made diagram and key. Doing so precludes the possibility of having any course member practice this valuable technique. Another method of producing the Step 3 diagram is preferable *only* because it shows course participants that at least one of them can easily perform this task. That method has sometimes

Design Format

Figure 2

*Step 3 Diagram
Interlinking Factors in the Case:
"Staff/Line Communication Blocks"*

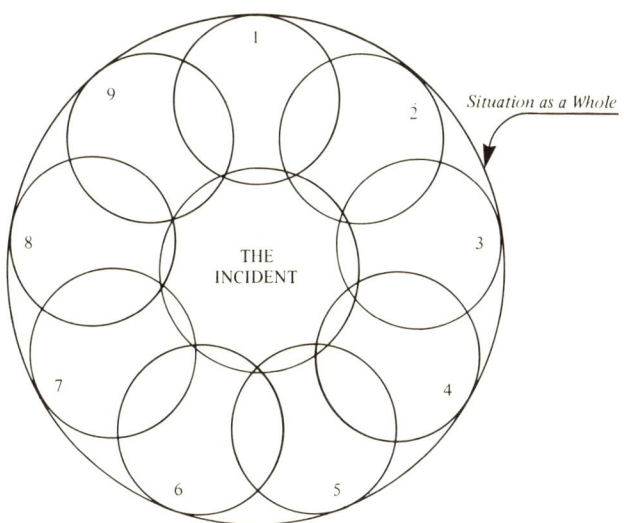

Key to Diagram:
1. BOMBARA AND HIS DEPARTMENT: duties; work relationships; reputation; departmental overload; staffing; delegation to Baker (at end of Incident).
2. BETTY: employment record; previous cooperation, achievement, and flexibility; ambition; indications of attitude and motivation.
3. THE SPECIAL PROJECT UNIT: its purpose; usefulness to 'our' division; high priority with top management; nature of work.
4. MR. MARCH: position and responsibilities; qualifications; personality; past action in the case.
5. MS. HARRIS: organizational responsibilities; personality; past action in the case.
6. OTHER PERSONNEL IN OUR DIVISION: especially Walker and Coit (their responsibilities and capabilities); clerks (in Sections A and B and in the Special Project Unit).
7. BAKER: organizational role; specific responsibilities including "general supervision" of three clerks temporarily reassigned to the Special Project Unit; past action in regard to Betty.
8. MANAGEMENT RELATIONSHIPS: March-Bombara; Bombara-Baker; March-Harris; Baker-Coit-Walker; Baker-Harris.
9. TIME FACTOR: It is now 3:30 p.m.; 'today' is Betty's fourth working day in the Special Project Unit; pressure for speed in that Unit; demand for an immediate replacement for Betty (tomorrow morning).

been undertaken on the initiative of some member who, perceiving the task as a good game, grabs the ball and runs off with it—completing the entire 'play' (unless restrained) with no cooperation from anyone else. However, to an inexperienced discussion leader, effective action by one course member may appear greatly preferable to no action by anyone—at the start of Step 3. Certainly, it's not a happy situation to have members of a study group just sitting there, saying nothing, because no one knows how to proceed. Sometimes, in PIP's earlier days, this is precisely what happened.

The next task is to make a key to the diagram. This part of the work may take five minutes or more. But one will find the time spent is well worth it. A carefully crafted key spells out sub-factors. Doing this helps to ensure that no significant part of any factual 'building block' will be forgotten when structuring the immediate decision for action to cope with the Incident.

Step 3 is completed when course members *boil down the whole case, temporarily, to a question*—single or multiple—for prompt decision. Many managers perform approximately this same task in their everyday work relationships. After a committee discussion, someone may say, "As I see it, this is what the whole thing boils down to."

Formulating an issue might seem an easy task to someone who has never tried to do it. But supervisory and managerial decisions have often failed to be useful because the questions they *answered* were not the ones that most needed to be *asked*. Moreover, many arbitrators have had serious difficulties in helping representatives of labor and management to agree on an issue which pinpoints the nature of their current dispute.

In formulating an issue for administrative decision, two dangers to avoid are : (1) simplistic thinking and (2) bias. For instance, in "Betty's" case, Baker might (unwisely) phrase

Design Format 37

the immediate issue like this: Should I say to Mr. Bombara: "How in hell can I 'take care of it' when I haven't a clue as to what's been going on over there?" Or (following Bombara's lead): "Shall I tell Coit and Walker immediately to select our best qualified clerk as Betty's replacement and then decide, later, how to discipline Betty?"

If a case student suggests some such oversimplified formulation of what is at stake 'here and now' in the case, a leader isn't infringing on the right of participants to think for themselves by asking: "Does everyone agree that this statement of the issue points toward a decision which would meet Baker's major organizational responsibilities right after the Incident?" Perhaps no one will follow this lead toward organization-minded thinking. In that event, a leader may wish to point to the diagram and key, asking: "If that were all there is to it, wouldn't we have been wasting our time factoring out all these interactive elements?" If even that hint doesn't work, a leader may decide—in connection with the first case analyzed—to make a positive suggestion. For instance: "Might it be more useful to put it this way: in Baker's organizational role, right after the Incident, (1) whom should I talk with; (2) in what sequence; and (3) with what objectives?"

When case students agree on some such statement of the immediate issue, they are headed toward a decision which (1) takes account of current organizational realities, yet (2) does not restrict action later—at the policy level—toward organization-wide goals.

What About a Coffee Break?

At about this point in a two-hour session, a discussion leader is likely to be confronted by a small, but not insignificant, question for administrative decision; namely: When shall we have the coffee break, and for how long?

Course members may now have been at work for about an

hour. But unless the time already spent on the case has been considerably more than an hour (and it shouldn't have been), a coffee break can be more productive if postponed until after the first suboperation in Step 4. (The reasons for that statement will soon become obvious.)

STEP 4: Decisions and Reasoning.

According to updated PIP practice, Step 4 is composed of four suboperations:

Suboperation (4a): Setting up opinion groups. This can be done quickly by inviting participants to make individual choices from a spectrum of possible decisions as to how the Incident might best be handled. (A range of options is displayed by the discussion leader.) Sometimes a few rugged individualists reject all proposed options. They form splinter groups (occasionally consisting of a single member). If these opinion groups can be set up before the coffee break, most participants go right on working during this free time. They spontaneously team up with like-minded members (usually in three or four subcommittees) to begin—

Suboperation (4b): Conferring in Separate Opinion Groups. The task of each such subcommittee is to bring out, to thresh out, and to consolidate reasoning which supports their mutual decision. (If any subcommittee consists of a minority of one, a member of the leading team may wish to ask if an additional member would be welcome. If accepted, the primary task of this second member is *not* to supply additional reasons, but rather to draw out the original member.)

Orderly discussion of differences, reinforced by attentive, continuous listening, is best assured if the first order of business, for each subcommittee, is electing a chairperson. The primary responsibility of the person in that role is to poll everyone in the opinion group. When all the different reasons have been stated, committee members can select the ones which seem most persuasive, and perhaps improve one or two of them by a little re-wording. During this time, either the chairperson or another committee member to whom this task has been delegated is expected to take brief notes. These notes should indicate not only the subcommittee decision, but also the final form of each supporting reason. At the end of Step 4, the notes will be given to the official observer to supplement whatever that individual was able to record while each group opinion was being presented. A final responsibility of the chairperson is supervising decision-making as to: (1) whether the subcommittee opinion is to be presented by a spokesperson or a role-player, and (2) who is to represent the group in either capacity.

Suboperation (4c): Presenting and Attending to Subcommittee Opinions. By paying close attention to each spokesperson and role-player, the group-at-large can get the benefit of a diversity of views as to how a given Incident might best be handled. But role-playing cannot fully reveal the reasoning that supports a given decision. That's the chief reason why the official observer needs notes which clearly show what was said in working out a reasoned decision that is presented by a role-player. (This additional material is given to the group-at-large later, in the written report.)

Some discussion leaders prefer to have subgroup opinions presented by spokespersons, rather than in role-playing. This is because a role-played interview usually takes a minimum of five minutes, while a competent spokesperson can present a reasoned decision in about two minutes. However, it can be argued that the disadvantage is more than counterbalanced by the fact that role-playing tests a player's ability: (1) in the role of a communicator, to 'sell' a given decision, and (2) in the role of a decision receiver, to respond 'in character,' yet with some flexibility, to another role-player. Many case students have found that it's much easier to state a reasoned decision, in relatively abstract terms, than it is to get it across, and to make it acceptable, to an individual who prefers some other solution.

If subgroups are to be represented by spokespersons *and* role-players, experience suggests scheduling speakers before players. When role-players come first, the audience is likely to suffer a sense of anti-climax as speakers start. This mood tends to lower the level of listening.

To illustrate both kinds of presentation, here are excerpts from a report on a discussion of the case: "Staff/Line Communication Blocks."

The spokesperson for one opinion group stated their view as follows:

> "First, we must immediately select a suitable replacement for Betty. (March has insisted on that.) But—
> "We can't find a suitable replacement until *after* we've got the facts as to what our girls do over there.
> "Obviously, the person to give us that information is Harris. But—
> "We can't get to Harris except through March. So—
> "We'd begin by talking with March."

That sounds like a realistic decision, doesn't it? As far as it goes. But it doesn't include any mention of who should break the news to Betty, where, and when, or whether there should be any effort to get her side of the story. Nor is there any reference to clearing with Bombara, by the end of the afternoon—when everything has been "taken care of"—for the time being.

At that same meeting, another subcommittee had decided to present essentially the same decision by role-playing. (The discussion leader played the part of Mr. March.) Here's the gist of that interview:

> BAKER (jauntily, over the telephone to Mr. March): "Hi, there. I'm Baker. George tells me that Betty hasn't been working out too well, and that you want a replacement. I wonder if you could spare me five minutes, so I could get a clear idea as to . . ."

Design Format 41

MARCH (interrupting, irritably): "Who in hell are *you*? And who is *George*? I can't waste time talking with people I don't even know. And all anyone *needs* to know about *Betty* is that she must be replaced, immediately!"

BAKER (in a more subdued tone): "I'm the Assistant Manager in the General Agency Contracts Division, and George is my boss. You've just been talking to him about a replacement for Betty. But we can't be sure of sending the best girl for the job unless we know exactly what our clerks do in your unit."

MARCH (snappishly): "There's no point wasting my time on trivialities. Just send us a good, dependable girl. The other clerks are working out all right."

BAKER: "Could you perhaps arrange to have Ms. Harris give me a few minutes?"

MARCH: "Now you've begun to make sense. Ms. Harris happens to be right here. I'll put her on."

BAKER then arranges (with Harris) to come right over and get the information he needs.

That interview illustrates the kind of difficulty that is likely to arise when a middle-level line manager attempts to communicate with top-level staff—in the person of an individual who is trained as a technical specialist—who has recently been put in charge of a special project which is of paramount importance to top management, and who takes little interest in fellow employees as human beings.

Time permitting, a second interview may be role-played. This one might be between Baker and Harris. (And this talk, too, may reveal some unsuspected communication blocks.) Or, some other opinion group may also have decided to interview March by role-playing. In that event, there are advantages in having the same person take the part of Mr. March, in both interviews. The second "Mr. Baker" should be asked to leave the room during the first interview. Otherwise 'his' portrayal might be unduly influenced by what happens to the first "Mr. Baker."

When course members are analyzing their first case, there may be no time for any role-playing. But, as the course progresses, Steps 2 and 3 can usually be taken more quickly, thus leaving more time for Steps 4 and 5.

By the third practice session, there may be enough time for—

Suboperation (4d): Comparing and Appraising Decisions and Presentations. If PIP participants are to derive full benefit from suboperations 4a through 4c, they need to compare and appraise the results of subcommittee work. Experience has shown that few individuals make such comparisons and appraisals on their own.

Questions which have often been asked and answered at this point in a PIP session, include:

• How do the *various decisions* stack up? One practical way to answer this question is by applying Maier's Risk Technique (Maier, 1952).

• In what respects, and for what reasons, were *some presentations* (by spokespersons or role-players) preferable to others? The answer to this question can be more useful to course members if they work it out for themselves. But a positive lead may be helpful. For example: "Let's begin by mentioning the strongest points in each presentation."

• What *is* the best way in which this Incident could have been handled? What actually was decided and done at the time? How did it work out? To the first part of this multiple question, a discussion leader who adheres to PIP policy would naturally reply: "In our opinion, there is no 'ONE BEST WAY' in which to cope with an incident where human beings and their interrelationships play an important part. Moreover, telling you *now* about the sequel to the Incident would interfere with your own case analysis. So, let's table that question for the moment."

STEP 5: Reflecting on Major Issues and Long-term Organization-wide Goals.

Having taken a close, hard look at specific facts of a case,

Design Format

and made short-term decisions about how to cope with an Incident, PIP practitioners are in a favorable position to answer a question often asked about case method in general: namely, "Since no two situations are ever alike, how can anyone hope to learn anything practical by studying cases?" Of course, specific facts are different in every case. But at the level of general ideas (e.g., principles, policies, long-term organizational goals), many cases are remarkably similar. If that were not true, how could executives learn so much in the hard school of experience? And serious case students, who are able and interested to educate themselves (in part) by vicarious experience, can acquire skills which help them to recognize and avoid many pitfalls before falling into them. The final phase of case analysis (by PIP) is taken at a relatively high level of abstraction. For this reason, there are significant advantages in having case students now promote themselves (collectively) to the role of a top executive. At this organizational level, decision-makers can make or revise policies to prevent the recurrence of troublesome situations. Even if the first four analytical steps have been taken by students in the role of an impartial arbitrator, the case situation doesn't come to an end with the arbitrator's 'final and binding' Award. On the contrary, top executives are then challenged to make a new beginning by preventive management.

A useful way for case students to practice policy thinking is by reviewing and appraising key elements in the case as a whole. Therefore, the culminating phase of case analysis begins with—

Suboperation (5a): Discussing Generalized Questions in Subcommittees. Each small group discusses one or more of the following topics:

1. What *negative factors* seem to have been accountable for difficulties in this case? (These *flaws* need *to be worked on.*)

2. What *plus factors* can be identified? (These positive forces can be used as resources *to work with*.)
3. What *needs for long-term action* are evident? (Such needs suggest ways *to work toward* organization-wide goals, at the policy level.)

In the first practice session, a majority of course members may flock to the 'flaws' question. But limiting one's view to shortcomings that jump to the eye is less productive, for development of executive potential, than digging out plus factors and considering them in relation to opportunities for long-term action. A hint that the second and third questions are more challenging than the first one is usually enough to attract outstanding students to those subcommittees. Or, some of the more rapid thinkers may wish to consider all three questions. In any event, 15-20 minutes can profitably be invested in this first suboperation.

Suboperation (5b): Considering Subcommittee Answers in the Group-at-Large. As spokespersons report subcommittee answers, the discussion leader records them, in three parallel columns, where everyone can see them. In the case "Staff/Line Communication Blocks," answers to the Step 5 starting questions have often included the following:

1. *Negative Factors*
    (a) *Way of managing* (and supervising)—by March, Bombara, and Walker overly production-centered; ignoring employee motivation; lack of follow-up by supervisors who retain "general" responsibility for temporarily reassigned clerks.
    (b) *Communication:*
       - *by March*; notably inadequate requisition for clerical personnel needed in the Special Project Unit.
       - *by Bombara*; no request for specifics at the time of March's requisition; stating (to his assistant) an unsupported assumption.

- *by Walker*; inadequate orientation of clerks who had been selected for a temporary reassignment.
  (c) *Time factor:* a crash program, with inadequate planning and coordination.
  (d) *Difficulties associated with organizational structure and formal relationships:* 'halo' effect for March set up a communication block between him and Bombara; role of 'project manager' creates difficulties of its own; division between "general" and "technical" supervision led to unmet supervisory responsibilities.

2. *Plus Factors*
   (a) Good. working relationships: Bombara-Baker; Baker-Coit-Walker; March-Harris.
   (b) Betty's capabilities and potential; adaptability and cooperative attitude (shown within the Division); excellent job performance (at least until four days ago).
   (c) Bombara's administrative ability and concern for this Division.
   (d) March's professional education, technical know-how, and enthusiasm for the Special Project.
   (e) Harris' technical knowledge and dedication to the Special Project.

3. *Needs for Long-Term Action*
   (a) More employee-centered way of managing.
   (b) Management development (even for supervisors whose responsibilities are regarded as purely technical).
   (c) More effective communication: e.g., in making and receiving requisitions for employees to be reassigned; in listening to a disturbed employee and taking account of inner motivation and outward signs of serious stress; regular and

frequent lateral communication among supervisors with joint responsibilities in work-related units.

(d) *Thoroughgoing planning* (for a high priority special project).

Suboperation (5c): Centering on Interrelationships of Factors. Five minutes or so (even longer, if the time schedule permits) can usefully be spent by the group-at-large in correlating various items in the three columns of answers. After the first practice session, this task can usually be accomplished by course members on their own, with the discussion leader merely drawing the connecting lines. Most of these lines are likely to indicate recognition of relationships between items in columns one and three. But at least a few lines should indicate that thoughtful participants took account of plus factors when they considered needs for action over the long haul.

Suboperation (5d): The Historical Footnote. Having taken an informed look ahead at the policy level, members of a case study group can now evaluate their own insight and foresight by applying the test of history. At this time, the leader reveals what actually was decided and done, immediately after the Incident in the case-for-the-day. Having briefly discussed the sequel to an Incident, members of a study group are ready for–

Suboperation (5e): Focusing on Major Issues. The answers in column three (still displayed for reference) contain the makings of a broad-gauged view as to what is at stake in the case–*over the long haul*. But, at least in connection with the first case, course members may need some help from a discussion leader, as well as from one another, in developing this view of a case. The kind of issue that now takes center stage is larger and 'longer' than the short-run issues that were considered in Step 3.

From the relatively impartial angle of a case student (or an

Design Format

arbitrator), these issues may be discerned as having been 'in' the Incident—implicitly—and also 'in' the case situation even before the Incident. But unlike issues for short-term decisions in any given case, *major issues* are not confined within the boundaries of any single case situation. As shown in Figure 3, at the policy level they reach out toward other situations— with respect to which they may be seen as common denominators. With reference to the case in which studying the "Betty" Incident was Step 1, major issues may be diagrammed as shown in Figure 3.

The kind of thinking required to identify and relate such issues represents a fourth stage in an alternate narrowing and broadening of view which is characteristic of PIP. In Figure 3 (as in Figure 2), readers will notice that the Incident is pictured as being in the center. That's where PIP students start. During Step 2, bits of information are brought out, to fill in the context—or total situation—within which an Incident developed. In Step 3, blocks of information are visualized in relation to one another; but attention is still confined (officially) to one case. (In the Step 3 diagram, the confines of that situation are indicated by the larger of the two circles.) In Step 4, the center of attention is again narrowed to the Incident (although its context supplies material for both decisions and reasoning). But in Step 5, students look beyond the confines of *any single case.* Interest now centers on scope for action indicated by the space between the second and third circles (in Figure 3), the area which is potentially richest in material for practical learning. (The largest circle is drawn with dotted lines to indicate that this boundary is not closed; a concept which is reinforced by the fact that the shape of major issues shows them extending beyond the outer circle.)

When the quest for generally applicable meanings constitutes the last step in a cycle of analysis which began by centering attention on one small incident, ideas developed

Figure 3

Diagram of Major Issues

CASE: "Staff/Line Communication Blocks"

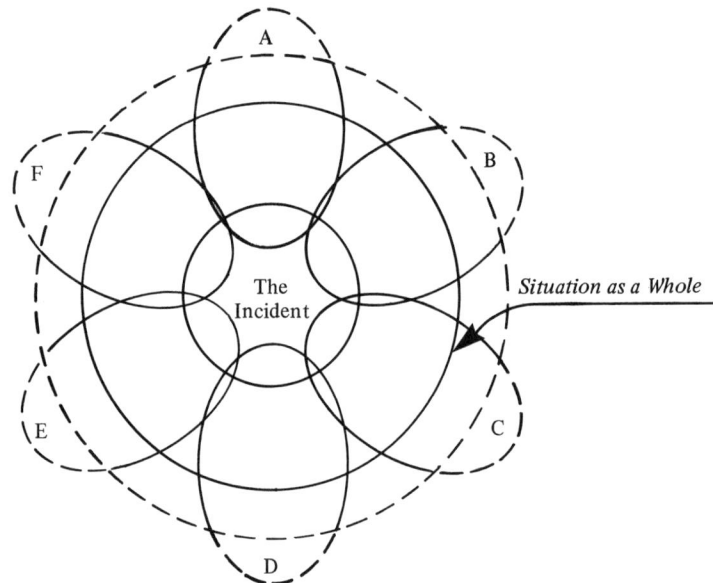

Key to Diagram:
A. Ways of Managing.
B. Staff/Line Relationships.
C. Interpersonal Communication: among management representatives, staff and line; and as an *interchange of views* in interviewing, counseling, transmitting information, requests, and orders.
D. Managerial Procedures: selection (for work assignments and reassignments); upgrading and downgrading; performance appraisals; merit increases; employee discipline.
E. Employee Motivation: Whose responsibility? Who can change inner motivation?
F. Planning for efficient coordination; implemented by effective communication.

Design Format

and decisions made during intermediary steps can be put into portable form—as generally valid propositions—for convenient carryover to everyday work. Spending 40 minutes or more in clarifying these general ideas offers students an opportunity to reap a rich reward from their previous work on a case.

However, if time runs out during a scheduled session, before Step 5 can be completed, a good second best can be offered by a competent observer-reporter. An approximation of the group view (to be evaluated during the first 'progress review' meeting) can be worked out from subgroup answers to the Step 5 questions that were displayed during the meeting. (That source material belongs in every report on group performance during case analysis.) The reporter's educated guess as to what the Step 5 diagram *would have been* makes a fitting end to such a report.

An Extension of Step 5 by Leaders

Soon after each meeting, the leading team should hold its own Step 5 session. This extra meeting (outside of course hours) can be especially fruitful for a 'first team.' By considering the usual Step 5 questions, a leading team can evaluate its own performance (before and during a group discussion) looking for ways in which to do a better job in the future.

B. How to Lead a Progressive Series of PIP Sessions

We have already mentioned that up-to-date PIP courses are structured as a progressive series. Changes from the initial structure have come about gradually, as the old PIP was fine-tuned, over the years. Several modifications were made to meet needs felt (and sometimes expressed) by course members. Other changes were made, on the Pigors' own initiative, to save time for tasks that seemed to us more productive.

As with any other kind of learning-teaching, the productivity of each PIP course depends, in part, on effective preparing, leading, and following to fit specific needs and opportunities offered by the situation in which the mutually reinforcing activities of learning-teaching are to be carried out. Specific preparations and plans (all interlinking) naturally differ according to such variables as: who is giving, and who is taking, the course; where it is to be given (e.g., in an academic or industrial setting); and how long each series is to be. Many readers of this text will be professional teachers, and members of their courses will, presumably, be full-time students, perhaps at the graduate level, and possibly with some previous experience in a business or industrial organization. However, other readers may be training directors or consultants, concerned with stimulating self-development in people who currently hold supervisory or managerial positions. For the latter group of readers, certain extra preparations are essential to ensure top management support and maximum benefits throughout the organization.

Anyone who has approved PIP, as a means for sizing up actual situations, would naturally consider the same (interrelated) factors which are recommended to all case students. The following suggestions, derived from the authors' experience, incorporate these same variables, and may be useful to teachers with little or no practical experience in leading case discussions.

• *The policy element* in a PIP course derives from the overall goal (to detect and develop managerial potential) and from various sub-goals toward which course members can make progress during a series of meetings. Policies also *show through* all the planning recommendations offered below and the guidelines for behavior (by teachers and students).

• *Time factor/human element.* What about scheduling? As already mentioned, *two hours* is the minimum length of time required for participants to do a thorough job in all five steps

Design Format 51

of the analytical cycle and in the special meetings (where emphasis is on "this case"—the situation of the workgroup itself). Two and one-half to three hours is an even better length of time for a PIP meeting, partly because it eases the pressure to get out production. A *weekly interval between meetings* allows time: (1) for all participants to assimilate and reflect on ideas and techniques which are new to them; and (2) for the official observer to write a thoughtful and thought-provoking report, which can then be distributed to course members at least three days before the next meeting.

In an academic setting, more serious difficulties may arise in connection with scheduling a *two-hour* session, *twice each week* (instead of the traditional one-hour meeting on alternate days, three times a week, which actually allows 50 minutes working time for each meeting). But during 25 years, the senior author made the necessary arrangements (with cooperation from members of the curriculum committee and from interested students at M.I.T.). So it can be done. A practical and congenial possibility for lengthening a session becomes a reality if enrollees voluntarily contribute their lunch hour to a twice-weekly, two-hour session. When a working lunch comes during the first hour, there's no need to fear that drowsiness will handicap anyone, even during the after-lunch hour. Listening to a lecture sometimes seems to induce sleep, especially right after lunch. But starting with a lively Incident and helping to develop it into a 'live' case, tends to keep students on their toes.

- *Decisions as to the length of each PIP course* should take account of PIP policy and the human element. How long does it take to learn what is offered in a PIP course, or how much money is management prepared to invest for this purpose? In an academic setting, the length of each course is normally predetermined for each semester. The number of meetings is great enough so that all course members can volunteer for *both* leading roles—if they so desire. There can also be at least one additional 'progress review' meeting. A good time for such a review is just before volunteers exchange leading roles. Incidentally, an added advantage is that there is no need to schedule interim or final examinations. Student performance can best be evaluated by consensus—among students and teachers—based on: (1) official and unofficial observation; (2) Discussion Plans made by volunteer leaders; and (3) the caliber of written reports turned in by volunteer observers.

In a business or industrial setting, it may be difficult to sell top management on the idea that, ideally, there should be at least ten or 12 meetings in every PIP course. Whatever the learning-teaching environment, there is need to consider the respective lengths of segments 2 and 5 (the demonstration and practice sessions, and the "Highlights" meetings). For example—

• The number of demonstration and practice sessions can be reduced from three to two. However, advantages of scheduling three sessions (as compared to two) include:

—For course members; more time, working with a professional leader, to become acquainted with PIP as a work method. This reduces the risk that some course member (having volunteered to function as a discussion leader with delegated responsibilities) will introduce a change in method which is incompatible with the general plan of PIP; e.g., omitting the summary, or cutting out Step 3, or merely doing only the last part of Step 3, or forgetting all about Step 5. A second advantage for course members is the opportunity to become better acquainted with one another. This can be a significant plus factor when it's time to team up in leading roles.

—For instructors, the third practice session offers more scope to model leading roles and to demonstrate a work method. It also gives a 'first team' more opportunity: (1) to become acquainted with course members—including those

who don't say a word (at first); and (2) perhaps to provide a bit of informal follow-up between meetings, for course members who seem overly talkative or unduly silent.

A preferred *sequence of meetings,* each with its own character and purpose, has already been outlined. Further details as to 'what's,' 'how's,' and 'why's' of this sequence are given below, starting on page 57.

* *Spatial/Human Planning.* Easy interaction among participants is a prerequisite for maximum progress in a PIP course. This goal can be attained only in a room where chairs and tables are arranged for *conferring.* Unless furniture is nailed to the floor, a lecture room can rapidly be converted into a conference setting by fashioning a horseshoe arrangement of seating so that everyone can easily see everyone else. (Tent cards, with names on both sides, also facilitate easy interaction among course participants.) PIP students also need table space on which to write and to spread out case material (of various kinds, including their own notes on what is done at each meeting. Chairs with writing-arms are less convenient for the latter purpose.). The room should be large enough so that subcommittees can confer in relative privacy. A plus factor is an adjoining room to which some small groups can withdraw from time to time (in Steps 4 and 5).

* *Environmental/Human Planning.* In selecting a conference room, other points to consider include: its accessibility; the likelihood of being able to meet in the *same* room each week throughout the course; controlled temperature; and absence of excessive noise from outside. When planning in a business organization for a *psychological climate* conducive to learning by group process, a special item for consideration is prevention of what can be the most disruptive kind of noise from outside, for example, telephone calls for a group member. Such a call may snatch a member from a meeting. At best it is distracting; and it may establish an undesirable precedent. If possible, a teacher should win agreement, at the

first meeting, that no participant is to take any outside calls during scheduled course hours—unless a dire emergency occurs, on a scale such that no deputy can cope with it.

• *Technical/Human Planning.* Among the questions in this category are:

—*How can instructors best prepare themselves to lead case discussions by PIP?* Reading about what others have done can be a useful preliminary. But, if possible, reading should be supplemented by first-hand experience as a participating member in at least one demonstration session. Functioning for even one meeting (better still, for several) as an official observer-reporter can be another excellent way to prepare for leading. Ideal preparation includes: serving as the continuing observer (on the first team) throughout most of a course, and then undertaking the role of discussion leader. These recommendations should not be taken to mean that people aren't up to the job until they have already had experience in all aspects of it. But, as in other kinds of responsible work, the more experience, the greater the probability of superior performance.

—*How can an instructor recruit a partner?* People who have ever tried to talk, listen, think on their feet, continually observe all members of a discussion group, and take notes—all at the same time—are in a position to appreciate the value of delegating some of these responsibilities to an able partner. Perhaps an instructor can secure the services of a permanent partner (in the person of a qualified and interested friend or spouse). Or, a former graduate may be enlisted—at least for the first three or four meetings. Another possibility, in a school where inter-disciplinary interaction is practiced, is to enlist a colleague from another department: Psychology? English? Current Events? Law? etc. At the graduate level, PIP can profitably be used to stimulate productive thinking by students in all these subjects. In a business or industrial enterprise, it should be easy to enlist a colleague from the

Design Format

personnel department. (Perhaps that individual might later give a PIP course.) Or, possibly, some personnel officer from another organization would jump at the chance to observe a PIP course in action.

—What about the number of participants in each course? This variable determines, in large measure, the opportunity for each member actively and frequently to participate at every meeting. For example, if there are more than 25 members in a course, individual participation must be severely limited; especially since—under such circumstances—aggressive members will make strenuous efforts to get more than their share of the action. Therefore, if more than 25 people sign up for a course, an instructor should try to persuade some of them to head the waiting list for the next course. However, fewer than eight course members unduly limits the range of views and diversity of opinions that are eminently desirable in a course which features practicing skills needed to integrate differences. Unless some way can be found to enroll at least 12 (preferably 15) students, the course should be postponed.

—How about the mix? When instructors are free to select candidates, they should try to include men and women; systems-minded people; and others interested primarily in management or in human relations; and members of different ethnic groups. The systems-minded people (perhaps math majors, actuarial students, or persons from an EDP department) can be counted on to provide the analytical skills called for by PIP. Having some representatives of line management, whose primary interest is in helping people to get out production, increases the probability of getting new case material from volunteer discussion leaders. Nowadays, it's not necessary to explain why it is desirable to include women and different races in a study group which discusses troublesome cases in human relations. This brings us to the next question:

—Which cases will work best as starters? The answer varies according to the situation in which PIP is to be used. In a business or industrial enterprise, it is essential *not* to begin with a case which is currently 'in the works.' It is risky to start even with a case 'from the works' (the organization in which cases are to be analyzed), *unless* the events happened so long ago that the people who were involved in them are no longer around. With issues, however, the reverse is true. For top value, short-term and long-term issues should be 'live.' Fortunately, this specification can be met: (1) by selecting from among many published cases (among these, see Paul and Faith Pigors: BNA, Inc., 1955, 1958, 1965), or (2) by studying current issues of *Labor Arbitration Reports* (The Bureau of National Affairs, Inc.), or (3) best of all, from an instructor's own experience in some organization. (Incidentally, the "Staff/Line Communication Blocks" case—used for illustrative purposes in this chapter—has proved its worth as a starter.)

—What items of handout material need to be prepared, in advance, for distribution at which meetings? The answer to this question depends on such variables as: the length and character of the course (for example, the number of cases to be prepared in advance should at least equal the number of meetings at which the instructor expects to take the leading role); whether the course is structured according to current PIP practice; and whether the instructor wishes to offer resource material such as is given in the Appendix to this text.

—Who will provide the looseleaf notebooks in which course members can file 'handouts' and various kinds of case material (including reports from official observers)? The senior author has always found it possible to convince top management to supply the notebooks, which contribute to maximum benefit for the organization as a whole.

Having made thoroughgoing plans and preparations, an

Design Format

instructor (preferably a teaching team) is ready to lead a case study group through a full-length PIP course. The general structure of a progressive series was outlined in the previous chapter. Here are further details as to 'what's,' 'how's,' and 'why's,' for each of the course segments.

SEGMENT 1: The Mutual Orientation Meeting

Advantages of mutual introductions, and of briefly discussing proposed goals for participants, have already been mentioned.

"Operation Springboard" (Op.S., for short). This mental exercise has proved both enjoyable and useful as a means to: (1) help all course members clarify assumptions and attitudes which are relevant for case study in human relations; and (2) initiate *discussion among participants* (thus demonstrating, from the very beginning, the expectation that course members can and will *learn from one another*). Here is how Op.S. can be used to achieve those objectives. (Copy in Appendix.)

While blank forms are being passed around, the discussion leader explains that this is *not a test*. It is merely an opinion survey and a basis for future discussion. Completed forms will be kept confidential, and—after being used to make a preliminary class profile—they will be returned.

Within eight minutes or so, individual opinions can be indicated on the form. Rapid thinkers—who are interested in words—can also edit some of the printed statements. Completed (*signed*) forms are turned in to the observer. During the next three or four minutes, the discussion leader can distribute a duplicate set of blank forms. These are for use as reference material during the ensuing discussion—the plan for which is now described to course members. Meanwhile, the observer is rapidly sorting the completed forms and listing the names of participants who indicated different opinions on at least two printed statements. (On the sample form, given on pages 96-97 of the Appendix, statements numbered four and seven have never failed to elicit clear-cut differences.)

Now the fun begins. Referring to the observer's lists, the discussion leader requests one participant, "A," to explain to another participant, "B," why he or she agreed (or disagreed) with a given statement. After listening to A's opinion, B explains the basis for a different view. Often, at this stage, participation spreads spontaneously, as others chime in to offer their views and *briefly to describe experiences* from which their opinions were derived.

Doing this much with Op.S. takes at least 20 minutes. If another 10-15 minutes can be invested in this exercise, small-group work can bring everyone into the act—orally. Each of three subcommittees can consider and report on one of the following assignments:

1. "Parody written statement # X so that no reasonable person could possibly agree with it."
2. "Edit (the same statement) so that, in your opinion, no reasonable person could disagree with it."
3. "Rewrite (the same statement) so that it seems to you a valid generalization."

A high point in this stage of Op.S. was the following parody of statement #7: "Everyone can be counted on to work much harder and faster, and continually to meet the highest standards of performance, if they are always given a lot more work than they could possibly do."

With or without this kind of small-group exercise, Op.S. can usefully be followed by:

A film. This part of the first meeting may take from 40 to 50 minutes. Its purposes are: (1) to test the perceptivity of course members; (2) to demonstrate the need for looking beneath outward behavior before trying to predict what someone will do next (a challenge which constantly confronts managers); and (3) to get a range of individual perceptions expressed. For the first and second purposes, the film should be a documentary (or at least approximately true-to-life) and should be divisible into four or five

Design Format 59

segments, with guided discussion in between. The Pigors have had favorable results with the *National Aircraft* film (Harvard University, Graduate School of Business Administration, 1959).

Each of these episodes should consist in, or contain, an incident during which at least one individual is portrayed as being under stress. After each film sequence, students are asked to predict (making an intelligent guess, based on observed facts and valid inferences) what the distressed person will do next. These guesses are immediately put to the test, as the next film sequence is shown. When many (or all) predictions turn out to be incorrect, course members should be informed that most people have made the same mistakes. This usually quiets negative feelings so that participants can give full attention to what may have been accountable for their errors. Was it having overlooked the fact that a person under stress often behaves in ways that are extremely difficult to predict? Was it perhaps also, in part, owing to having underestimated the power of inner motivation? A film which draws attention to such facts-of-feeling makes an excellent transition from initial orientation to—

The beginning of induction. Toward the end of the first meeting, it is time to explain what will be expected of PIP participants, technically, during each exercise of case analysis. A natural start for such induction is to refer to some "incident" in the film which has just been shown. A teacher naturally selects the incident which would seem most promising, if it were to be used as a launching pad for fact-finding questions. (For example, in the *National Aircraft* film, a "natural" is the scene where the plane catches fire.)

Then, using tearsheets or an overhead transparency, a teacher can run through PIP's analytical cycle. There is no need for course members to take notes during this explanation. Trying to carry on both activities at the same time tends to result in incomplete notes and diluted listening. Instead, toward the end of the first meeting, a teacher can distribute a one-page outline of the five analytical steps (along with samples of a case summary and a Step 3 diagram, which will also serve as general guides for future analytical work). When this material is *reviewed after* having listened to a concise oral explanation, it is likely to be more useful than either a written or oral explanation could be by itself. Furthermore, this practice illustrates the importance of good timing. If the written material is distributed during the initial explanation of the analytical steps, course members are tempted to read the material then and there, an activity which inevitably distracts their attention.

Closing the first meeting. In a session of two (or more) hours, there should be time enough at the end for a few questions from course members. But if there aren't any questions, this needn't worry a teacher. With or without questions, the meeting can be ended on a positive note. For example, it is always possible to congratulate participants on at least some of what has been said and done. Thus, a teacher may say (in effect): "You have had quite a workout today. And some of you may be wondering why, as members of a case study group, your varied activities didn't include analyzing a case. You will be doing so, at the next meeting—directly after a brief report from my partner on today's meeting. Meanwhile, if you can study the written material you have received today, our first exercise in case analysis will go more smoothly than it otherwise could." Probably it can also be said, on the basis of observed facts: "My partner and I have already spotted people here who are evidently qualified to take leading roles (if they have time) later in the course. If anyone would like to move up the 'organizational ladder' as soon as next week, by joining our team as an associate observer, please speak to one of us today."

SEGMENT 2: Demonstration and Practice Sessions

If a given course must be limited to eight or nine meetings in all, there can probably be only two practice sessions. The previous chapter contained several recommendations for leading these meetings. Here are a few additional suggestions:

• Begin with a brief *oral* report (from the first observer) on the introductory meeting. *Plus* factors of such a start include:

—*Hearing from the staff member* on the "first team" indicates what kinds of notes that individual has been (and will be) taking. It, therefore, gives participants some idea as to this member's role and personality.

—An *informal report* reinforces the tone already set by the discussion leader.

—A report which emphasizes *what was done well* makes an encouraging prelude to a meeting in which course members will encounter some difficulties. Examples of productive performance which can be reported may include: (1) the number of persons who did some *written editing* of Op.S. (sometimes as many as 11 out of 20 members present have edited five or six of the ten statements); (2) *notable contributions* during discussion of an Op.S. statement or of the film; and (3) evidences of *productive interaction* among members of the group-at-large, or in subcommittees.

As previously mentioned, three demonstration and practice sessions (rather than two) give course members more time to get the hang of the technical method, and to improve their acquaintance with one another. Moreover, six hours of practice, spread over two or more weeks, permit a teacher adequately to demonstrate PIP's few ground rules and to introduce more group dynamics techniques. The additional meeting also allows time for course members to assimilate three reports from the first observer. In these reports, an observer documents signs of progress, for example spontaneous responses to the picture of group work in Step 2 (given in the standard fact-finding table); and action taken on a teacher's suggestion that the most appropriate criterion for selection of a chairperson or role-player is that someone has not yet had an opportunity to demonstrate the required skill rather than convincing evidence that certain individuals already have a high degree of the abilities needed for serving in these capacities.

Especially in the first few sessions, instructors giving a PIP course should bear in mind that:

- What they *say* and *do* (the outward signs of 'who' they are) set the tone, and establish precedents which tend to influence members of a study group throughout a course. In this respect, an item of first importance is that teachers demonstrate their integrity. One such demonstration can be given when course members, on arriving at the second meeting, find Op.S. papers—unmarked—at each place. An observant teacher can almost hear the unspoken response: "So this really *was* an opinion survey and not a test."

- Not all explanations given at the first meeting will have been fully understood by every course member. Nor will written material have been carefully studied by everyone before the second meeting. Therefore, it is advisable to allot a little time during the first exercise in case analysis (possibly even in the second) for reviewing previous explanations.

- If any mini-incidents occur during the demonstration and practice sessions, an able discussion leader can demonstrate how a difficulty in human relations may be transformed into an advantageous opportunity. (For example, if some overly aggressive participant constantly speaks up without waiting to be recognized, a teacher can tactfully draw this difficulty to the attention of the group and enlist their help in overcoming it.)

- *Written reports on group performance* should: be distributed promptly after each practice session; be as complete as is compatible with time constraints; and be sufficiently thought-provoking to—

Design Format 63

—challenge the inner motivation of students, and
—serve as approximate models of what will be expected from other observers (each of whom is responsible for contributing to the cumulative record of performance in this ongoing situation).

• A timely moment for an encouraging word from the discussion leader comes toward the close of the first practice session. Unless this has been a one-shot demonstration, for seasoned executives, it is rarely possible to distribute orchids for brilliant performance at every step. What always has been possible, in the authors' experience, is to comment appreciatively on:

—useful contributions (by some members) at various steps of the analytical process;
—widespread participation, at least in fact-finding; and
—the cooperative spirit shown in tackling a variety of assigned responsibilities, many of which are difficult until they become familiar.

A teacher may properly add a reference to: (1) *the fact* that minimum standards have been established 'today' by and for this study group; and (2) *the expectation* that these standards will be raised during succeeding meetings. (They always have been.)

Another 'closing' duty is to help course members start preparing for the time when some of them will volunteer as leaders-for-the-day. Starting 'now,' ambitious participants who wish to gain full value from the course should begin asking themselves, "Have I had some experience which might be interesting and instructive for members of this group to analyze *as a case?*" Or, "What might I learn, and contribute, if I were to volunteer for the job of an official observer-reporter at one meeting?" (Often, a teacher can help potential teammates get together—perhaps because, in a private conversation, someone has expressed interest in volunteering as an observer-reporter.) Plans for the next meeting—an interim 'progress review'—can usefully be mentioned at the very end of the *last* practice session. A general statement can be made specific by distributing copies of proposed goals and an agenda for that meeting. As course members study that proposal, review written reports on group performance, and reflect on their own experiences during previous meetings, they are getting ready for a kind of participation which is needed to attain the two-fold objective of the progress review: the first meeting at which *the whole group will focus primarily on "this case"* (the ongoing situation of the study group itself).

SEGMENT 3: An Interim "Progress Review"

By this time, members of the "first team" should have been able to identify natural leaders in the study group. Thus, before subcommittees start on the job of appraisal, outstanding course members may be asked to join different subgroups. If any participants have consistently demonstrated a negative attitude, a teacher may request that not all of them work in the same subcommittee.

Analyzing and Appraising Basic Variables in "This Case." The main business of the meeting begins when subcommittees take stock of accomplishments to date and plan for further progress toward agreed-upon goals for the course. Because this analytical thinking is done in small groups, every course member has ample opportunity to participate. During 30 minutes or so, each subcommittee can consider at least one basic variable. The recommended approach combines Steps 2 and 5 to bring out facts-as-perceived (including facts-of-feeling); to clarify them as positive or negative factors in the situation; and then to view them as indicators of action needed to attain long-term goals for the course as a whole.

Committee Reports. Another half hour is needed to hear, and thoroughly discuss, reports from chairpersons. A teacher should not be surprised if some committee reports reveal

Design Format

negative attitudes. That's par for the course, at this stage. A great advantage is that chairpersons can report negative feelings (which might otherwise be suppressed) without indicating whose feelings they are. Once such attitudes have been brought into the open, it may be possible to change the work situation, or someone's perception of it, so that a negative attitude can be modified. Moreover, it often happens that a negative comment from one spokesperson is contradicted by another speaker. Here are a few sample comments.

Negative Comments
1. "The first meeting to orient us was unnecessary."
2. "For a course like this, we need much more orientation than we got."
3. "The style of leadership has been too authoritarian."

Positive Comments
1. "The Op.S. exercise and the film, at the first meeting, were good. They helped us to understand what would be expected of us in this course."
2. "Leadership has been excellent; offering some guidance, but not in an authoritarian manner."
3. "The fact that we're under pressure to get out production on every case isn't all that bad. Supervisors seldom have as much time as they need when they must make decisions and go into action."

Closing the Meeting. At the end of this meeting, a teacher can explain the purpose of the upcoming working session. Presumably, at least one volunteer leader (possibly two or three) will already have signed up. All course members should be urged to attend the next meeting, even if they plan not to volunteer for either leading role.

Immediately after official adjournment of the "Interim Progress Review Meeting," members of the "first team" can perhaps begin to function in some new aspect of their multiple role. For example, will there be an edited Incident to return to a volunteer leader who submitted it in draft form the previous week?

The written report on the 'Progress Review' meeting summarizes group decisions regarding proposed innovations (if any); lists names of volunteer discussion leaders (possibly even teams) already signed up; gives dates chosen by those leaders; and indicates whatever dates remain open for other volunteers.

SEGMENT 4: The Working Session

This meeting has proved advantageous in various ways—including the availability of 'first-team' members to give advice (upon request). The usual activities of this meeting are:

Signing up teammates. A full roster of volunteer teams has rarely been completed before the fifth meeting of a course. This is one reason why all course members should attend the working session. Many of those who did not expect to take either leading role have found, at the start of this meeting, that they wish to join a team after all (perhaps in the role of a 'free' observer, as described below). According to the wishes of team leaders, and the availability of volunteer 'staff' members, each team may have one observer-reporter, or perhaps two. When there have been two, one of them has sometimes been a 'free' observer. This role was created for course members who are interested in functioning as observers (during one meeting) but who lack the time needed to write a report. Often, however, teams have included two official observer-reporters; each being responsible for half of the job.

Conducting a trial run on a case and a Discussion Plan (each team working by itself). Such a test flight offers a variety of opportunities for a kind of teamwork which can pay off for the whole study group. For instance, a *volunteer discussion leader* can try out, and perhaps improve, a written Incident and any other parts of the Discussion Plan that have already been drafted. A leader's ability to answer questions briefly, objectively, and concisely can also be pretested.

Design Format

While *observer-reporters* are joining in the trial run, they too can benefit. Usually this workout is their first opportunity to: (a) acquire information on the leader's case; (b) make their own analysis of it; and (c) become thoroughly familiar with the leader's plan for group work on the case. Such information is virtually a prerequisite for efficiency on the Big Day, by an official observer who needs to be *freed from* all necessity to be briefed on the case and the Discussion Plan, in order to be *free for* giving undivided attention to the case situation which will then be unfolding.

Even individuals who do not volunteer for any leading role need not waste their time during a working session. One way to challenge their interest is for a teacher to ask them whether they have had some experience which they might present to this study group, as a case, if: (a) the material were less sensitive; or (b) they had time to do the necessary preparation. Course members with either of these handicaps can draft an Incident; jot down a summary of key facts (all of which will be kept strictly confidential by members of the "first team"); and do as much other work on their cases as time permits. Over the years, many PIP participants have become so enthusiastic about their 'might-have-been' cases that they continued to spend time on them even after the working session.

In the unlikely event that a few course members don't fit into any of the above categories, they can either read descriptions for the two leading roles (for better appraisal of performance by leaders) or leave the meeting early.

During the time when volunteer teams and 'loners' are at work, members of the "first team" can move about the room—separately—pausing to answer any questions and to see how preparations are coming along. The task of making an adequate Discussion Plan can rarely be completed at a single session. But usually the team which is to take the lead the following week has made a start on this planning before the working session. If so, a teacher may need only to check with the team leader; making sure that necessary arrangements have been made for duplicating all material which is to be distributed to group members. (In an academic setting, a volunteer leader's plan for getting material duplicated may consist in delegating that responsibility to a teacher—who, in turn, delegates the assignment to a secretary.)

After all such preparations have been completed, the study group is ready to begin what will be—at least for volunteer leaders—the most crucial meetings in the whole course.

SEGMENT 5: "Highlights of the Week"

When a study group is rich—in respect to time and the caliber of its members—there may be as many as four of these meetings (in an in-house course) or ten to 12 (during an academic semester). During each of these sessions, volunteer leaders can count on a high degree of attentiveness from their associates. But not all of this attention will be directed to the case that is being presented for discussion. Members who expect to take the lead in the immediate future may be chiefly concerned with such issues as: What is this leader doing that seems to work well? What innovations and what kinds of behavior (if any) seem to be unproductive?

The Multiple Role of a Teacher or Teaching Team

During the sessions when the more obvious leadership responsibilities are being undertaken by volunteers, what about the "first team"? (For simplicity in writing and reading the following paragraphs, it is taken for granted that a team, and not merely an individual, retains accountability for the course as a whole.)

As each volunteer team moves up front, for one meeting, members of the "first team" take a back seat—so to speak. They now occupy the places left vacant by the acting deputy leaders. But it is useless to pretend that any rearrangement in

Design Format 69

seating can erase all the experience and skills acquired by teachers. Nor does it absolve the "first leaders" from accountability for performance by course members during each series of meetings. The ways in which members of a "first team" meet their executive responsibilities can be a significant factor in determining the kinds and degrees of learning available to PIP participants. Executive responsibilities of "first" leaders can be subdivided into "do's" and "don't's." The "do's" include providing supportive management in such roles as:

• *Representative of group purpose:* consistently demonstrating, by all they say and do, a proper degree of objectivity, sensitivity, and team spirit.

• *Consultant-coach:* for instance, (1) by answering a volunteer leader's questions as to some technique of group dynamics which might be tried out, or on how to prepare and use a standard Discussion Plan for group work by PIP. (Such a Plan has five sections, corresponding to PIP's five analytical steps. It may also be helpful to prepare a single abbreviated "Fact-Sheet" for reference.) Naturally, most of this coaching and consulting is carried on behind the scenes. In public, deputy leaders should (as much as possible) be visibly on their own. However, there are exceptions to this general rule. The only potentially disruptive exception must be made if a volunteer leader starts answering some question as to what happened *after the Incident.* It is understandable that inexperienced leaders, on their toes to answer each question that is asked, may get caught in the trap set (inadvertently) by someone who asks such an 'out-of-order' question. But if some volunteer leader starts to blurt out (in Step 2) any information on the sequel to the Incident, a teacher is obligated to remind the study group that, according to PIP, this information is reserved for Step 5. Therefore, whatever may accidentally have been said, about the latter part of the case, should be treated as off the record. However, any accidental disclosure of this sort gives course members an opportunity to learn for themselves the reason for the rule of postponement. Declaring something 'off the record' doesn't erase that information from anyone's mind. On the contrary, the untimely information inevitably influences thinking during Steps 4 and 5.

• Another exception to the private-coaching rule is sometimes worth making in connection with group discussion of a *corporate policy*. But this exception *merely supplements* behavior by a volunteer leader, instead of implicitly criticizing it, and is usually made at a deputy's request. If a policy aspect of the case-for-the-day has neither been included in the experience of a volunteer leader, nor covered during preparatory coaching, and *if* no other course member is fully informed about the policy in question, then the 'first' leader can usefully supply information as to the general thrust of corporate policies in that area.

• *Pinch-hitter.* Sometimes a volunteer teaching team can't make it on The Day. Perhaps no other team can take that date on the spur of the moment. Therefore, teachers should always be ready to serve as replacements. Extra case material (written into complete Discussion Plans) should always be on tap for use in the event of a last-minute cancellation by a volunteer discussion leader. Or, if a volunteer observer drops out, a teacher—who usually functions as a discussion leader—may be glad to get a new angle on the study group by taking on the job of official observer-reporter for one meeting.

• *Continuing observer-appraiser.* This two-fold executive responsibility remains undiminished, for members of a 'first team,' throughout each PIP course. The fact that a succession of deputies shares certain specific responsibilities increases the *scope of accountability by the 'first' leaders*. Essential items for the private review held by a teaching team after every meeting now include: behavior by each deputy; and observable results of that behavior (in responses by other course members).

Design Format

In considering the 'gold reserve' represented by executive aspects of a teacher's role, the other side of the coin should not be overlooked. This side reflects undesirable kinds of behavior. For instance, teachers:

—Should *not tell* a volunteer discussion leader how to prepare for group work on a case. (A written role description can be more complete and is more impersonal. However, as noted above, consultation—at a volunteer's request—may be a positive contribution.)

—Should *not instruct* a volunteer observer-reporter as to what is expected of a participant in that role. (A written role description, supplemented by two or three written reports from the first observer, should provide ample instruction—unless, as previously mentioned, an observer asks for advice on some special matter.)

—*Should not charge to the rescue* of a volunteer discussion leader who is having difficulties with group members, or occasioning difficulties for them—*unless,* in a teacher's judgment, public coaching is absolutely necessary (as in the case of the out-of-order question noted above).

—*Should not be among the first to ask questions* during Step 2 (although a few questions that open up new territory can be useful IF ASKED after it becomes apparent that no one else is going to explore that area of the case).

—*Should not call for a summary*—either interim or final.

—*Should not volunteer to join any subcommittee* (in Steps 4 or 5), though being ready to accept all such invitations. However, the two 'first' leaders should not both serve on the *same* subcommittee.

—*Should not accept the role of chairperson, spokesperson, or role-player for any subgroup.*

—*Should not even try to impose their own opinions or reasons,* while decisions for short-term action are being developed (although there can be no reasonable objection to having teachers state their reasoning, when it's their turn to be polled on a subcommittee).

If teachers have discussed a deputy leader's case, in advance, to the point where they *know about the sequel to the Incident,* they:

—*Should not reveal any of that information.* They may even have to pass up the chance to state their opinion (in Step 4), if doing so would entail giving away information which will not be made available to the group-at-large until Step 5. (Such an unofficial, high-level leak would give one subcommittee—possibly two—an unfair advantage. It would also take the wind out of the leader's sails—in Step 5.)

—Should *not say much* during subcommittee deliberations at the start of Step 5, and *not* make more than one suggestion as to a major issue to be included in the Step 5 diagram.

—*Should not forget that at the end of a 'Highlight' Meeting,* a deputy is likely to be waiting for a public word of praise. If no such word is spoken, executive silence may be interpreted by the deputy as meaning: "You didn't do much of a job." In that respect, what is true for managers applies to PIP teachers too; a word of approbation, spoken too late and in private, can't undo the damage done to morale by untimely silence in public.

Getting Ready to Return to Regular Roles

Before the last "Highlight Meeting," a teacher can request a few minutes of closing time to explain the final session and distribute copies of proposed goals and an agenda for that crucial meeting.

'Highlights' conducted along such lines can yield a considerable measure of learning—for teachers as well as for students. But that's not all there is to it. *Clarifying* what has been learned is a necessary preliminary to *keeping it in mind*—so that, as opportunity offers, what has been learned can be practiced. Therefore, a PIP course is completed by—

SEGMENT 6: A Final Stock-taking and Planning Session

A general description of this meeting was given in the previous chapter. To 'get down to cases' here, we add a few specifics.

An appropriate start for the culminating meeting in a PIP course is to make a re-run of Operation Springboard. What differences in attitudes and assumptions will show up this time, as having come about during the series of meetings? Naturally, a second attitude survey can be valid *only* if course members: (1) indicate their current views *on the same written statements* that were presented to them before; and (2) do so *without referring to the previously completed forms* (presumably now filed in notebooks). For the latter purpose, the re-run is not specified in the proposed agenda for this meeting.

During the first subcommittee conferences (which *are* specified as an agenda item), a teaching team can enter the latest Op.S. results on the group profile which was made after the mutual orientation meeting (at the beginning of the course). A little later in this final meeting, significant changes can be reported to course members. (A suggested timing is given below.)

Subcommittee conferences and reports. Three small groups can now be set up. They may be composed of participants who have functioned (1) as *discussion leaders,* or (2) as *observer-reporters.* (3) A third subcommittee consists of those who now volunteer to serve as *overall evaluators.* Half an hour of conferring has always yielded an interesting mix of reports on experiences during the course. The following sample reports of student experiences are typical of those that have most frequently been made. They are included here to indicate the flavor of the 'summary' meeting in a PIP course.

—*A plus factor reported by discussion leaders:* "Being leaders taught us the nuts and bolts of PIP more thoroughly than we had learned [them] before."

—*A negative report from discussion leaders:* "Preparing our cases took too long; about five hours, for most of us. There has to be a better way." (The Pigors team responded to this comment by instituting the working session in subsequent courses.)

—*A benefit reported by observer-reporters:* "Making the Fact-Finding Table showed us that people tend to persevere along the line of questioning with which they start out. Most of them don't follow other people's leads—to explore the whole case."

—*A flaw noted by observer-reporters:* "A one-shot experience in this job isn't enough. We didn't really know what to look for."

—*An appraisal by observer-reporters:* "It was a big help to have two observer-reporters."

—*A report from evaluators:* "Some of the changes weren't good. When we got brief [oral] evaluations of our performance, at the end of a meeting, they were hasty and superficial."

After considering such comments, two items remain on the agenda for the final session: (1) returning to students, and briefly reporting on results of, the Op.S. re-run and (2)—if time permits—

Considering Major Issues. In the Pigors' experience, some of the same major issues have always been identified as significant for long-term action, in several (or all) of the cases discussed. To clarify these issues, at the end of a course, it works well to have three or four subcommittees (each with the same assignment) and to have at least one discussion leader and one observer-reporter in each subgroup. From subcommittee reports, the group-at-large can make a composite diagram. Figure 4 is typical.

Reflecting on the Course as a Whole
Instructors who have presided over reflective case analysis

Design Format

Figure 4

A Composite Step 5 Diagram

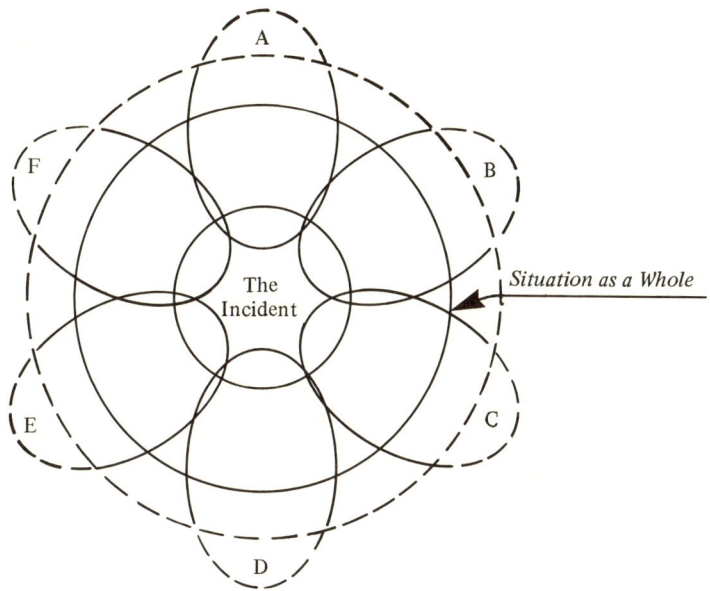

Key to Diagram:
  A. INTERPERSONAL COMMUNICATION: "Effective communication is needed among managers, and between managers and their subordinates. Listening is essential."
  B. STYLE OF MANAGING: "This factor influences the behavior of subordinates. Most managers need to be less production-centered and more people-oriented."
  C. ORGANIZATION STRUCTURE: "Formal relationships affect communication."
  D. INFORMAL RELATIONSHIPS: "Managers should try to learn what these are and should always take them into account."
  E. EMPLOYMENT PROCEDURES: "Selection, placement, induction, and training should all be done carefully. And there should be continuing follow-up. Progress reviews should be held often and regularly."
  F. PROMOTION POLICY: "Technical people need more opportunity for advancement. Delegation is an effective preparation for upgrading and promotion."

can feel assured that the course will continue to be productive. Moreover, this kind of group leadership (with considerable delegation and supportive management) entitles teachers to the satisfaction of knowing that they have passed a test formulated many centuries ago by the Chinese philosopher, Laotsu:

> .... of a good leader, who talks little,
> When his work is done, his aim fulfilled,
> They will all say, "We did this ourselves."

References

Harvard University, Graduate School of Business Administration, Soldiers Field, Boston, Massachusetts, 02163, Audio-Visual Department. Film: *National Aircraft,* 1959.

Maier, N.R.F. *Principles of Human Relations; Applications to Management.* New York: John Wiley and Sons, Inc., 1952, pp. 62-86.

The Bureau of National Affairs, Inc. *The Pigors Incident Process: Case Studies for Management Development. Series I: A Practical Course in Industrial and Human Relations for Foremen and Middle Management,* 1955; *Series II: Federal-State-Local Government Cases, 1958; Series III: White Collar Cases,* 1965.

IV.

OUTCOMES

PIP outcomes—for students, teachers, and the sponsoring organization—are directly related to inputs by all concerned. The more anyone in a study group (including a teacher) puts into the learning-teaching-group-making process, and the more support is given by the sponsoring organization, the greater the benefits all around.

It is no accident that the favorable results noted below tally so closely with the Pigors' goals for a PIP course. PIP was expressly designed to enable people to achieve significant results which are theoretically attainable by case method. Over the years, experience has suggested many modifications which make it increasingly easy for course members—with the will to experiment and to work—to achieve proposed goals.

However, many of PIP's outcomes are at least partly intangible. (Specific examples are given below, mostly under group process.) Some interim outcomes, for individual students, are temporarily invisible. (For example, when a subcommittee comes up with a closely reasoned opinion, teachers don't know—unless they have listened in—who did the work which went into that product. Also, attitudinal changes-in-the-making don't show up until—or unless—they break through in outward expression.) Moreover, potential outcomes are subject to a number of variables:

- *Total length of exposure to PIP* and time spent in job rotation (getting a range of experience in different roles).
- *Individual differences in students* (such as inner motivation, including ambition to learn, willingness to change, stage of maturity and of experience at the start of a course, and current degree of intelligence and perceptivity).
- *Individual differences in teachers* (style of teaching, degree of interest in encouraging learning, and willingness to accept criticism and to try experiments).
- *Freedom granted* by the sponsoring organization for expression of negative attitudes by course members toward organizational procedures and practices and for follow-up by teachers (if course members criticize the organization).

The unique mix of these variables in any given course may produce favorable or unfavorable conditions for self-development during group work and for changes of attitude.

Because attitudes are strongly affected by daily work experiences, outside of course hours, these experiences are another crucial variable. Changes that come *after* a PIP course cannot always be attributed to learning achieved during a course. For example, when outstanding course members are rapidly promoted to high organizational levels, who is to say that this outcome would not have occurred anyway? Some PIP graduates have expressed the opinion that PIP played a large part in their advancement. But such a statement is merely an opinion. Certainly, other factors also played a part—such as the inherent caliber of the individual, as well as promotion policy and job opportunities offered by the organization. Even if all subjective statements about advancement did match the facts, relatively few are reported, years later, to a former teacher, who may no longer be easily accessible.

Granting, then, that many outcomes of PIP are intangible, and that many remain unknown to teachers, let's look at some results that *are* observable and subject to verification.

Immediate Outcomes

When PIP is compared with the lecture method, differences in immediate results are dramatic. Teachers who have been accustomed to lecturing (and to reflecting on responses by their students) may be amazed and delighted at the intensity of participation evoked by a PIP session. This heightened response is typical, even at a first meeting. Perhaps the session is a demonstration for 100 persons or more. If so, the only difficulty may be to arrange adequate opportunities for even half of those who wish to speak. Or, perhaps the first exposure to PIP comes at a mutual orientation meeting such as was described in Chapter III. In either kind of setting, at least three immediate outcomes are predictable:

- A large majority, often everyone present, will find the experience stimulating and enjoyable.
- They will pitch in and work (to the extent that size of class, length of time, and a teacher's ingenuity make active participation possible).
- The individual response elicited by PIP's built-in pull will mean that even one experience will make an enduring impression on PIP participants. (For instance, many people exposed to a single PIP session—perhaps as a part of an AMA-sponsored management development course—have spoken about it to the senior author 20 or more years afterwards.)

But one PIP session, however skillfully led, and however enthusiastically responded to, is unlikely to result in lasting changes of attitudes and habits. Having stated that general proposition, it should be noted that there are exceptions. One of these was revealed by a senior executive who had volunteered to lead the first case discussion in a PIP course. His subsequent comment to the course director was: "You know, I learned more about conference leadership from that one experience than from all I ever read about it."

In addition to the immediate outcomes of using PIP, other significant results can be expected to show up after two or three meetings.

Interim Results: Evidence of Progress Toward Sub-Goals

Toward the end of a three-day conference, or after two or three practice sessions in a full-length course, an alert observer can see signs of changes in perceptivity, attitudes, and cognitive skills such as these:

- *Paying close attention to a small-scale, troublesome incident—regarding it as an early warning of potentially serious difficulties.*
- *Learning how to read for underlying meanings, and to listen for what speaks in a person*—below the level of spoken words. (What meanings can be read between the lines of a written document? What might be the significance of an unusual choice of words and of a given manner and tone in speaking or writing?)
- *Becoming increasingly adept in using certain control mechanisms,* as precautions against making snap judgments or simplistic decisions. For example,

  —Applying a systematic search pattern to 'get around' in an unfamiliar situation, or to re-evaluate a familiar one (a precaution against overlooking any significant area of a case, or underestimating the effect of some basic variable).

  —Working toward a 'multiple inside view' of a human relations difficulty: trying to see it from the angle of each individual who plays a key role in the situation, and to understand why some of those who are emotionally caught up in it might have 'reason' to behave 'unreasonably.'

  —Boiling down essential items (from a report or a discussion) and organizing them into an orderly,

concise, yet comprehensive action-pointed summary.
—Seeing relationships among key facts and weighing their relative meanings-for-action.
—Objectively formulating—*as a question for decision*—the nuts and bolts of a summary (issue formulation and factoring out sub-issues which need to be answered in an upcoming decision).

Gains in Interpersonal Relationships and Group Process

Progress in skills of human relations is often difficult to pin down and document. Indeed, many course members may not even notice this aspect of their progress, unless evidence of it is reported to them by observers. Examples of interim interpersonal outcomes are changes in such matters as:

- The nature of greetings, good-byes, and other small talk. These exchanges rapidly become more friendly. If the situation becomes tense at any time, a humorous comment by a participant may help course members to relax. Often, people who were relative or utter strangers at the start of a PIP course, find that they are making new friends after a few discussion meetings. A friendly attitude is characteristic of any encounter in which participants continue to engage in free discussion.
- A marked decrease in "dismissal reactions" (Lee, 1954) and a corresponding increase in responses that show mutual acceptance. (Observable signs of this change include: fewer interruptions or flat contradictions, and more instances of opinions expressed *as opinions*—spontaneously offered for discussion rather than stated as indisputable facts.)
- Natural leaders soon stand out—some of them as early as the first meeting. As these outstanding people use their knowledge and skills in the service of group

goals, other favorable outcomes—for all concerned—come into being. Among the latter are:
- The beginnings of genuine team relationships—as the first volunteers work together, preparing to do some of the leading.
- Experimentation—outside of class—with PIP as a discussion method for problem-solving. This is one of the most significant kinds of interim outcomes.

Benefits for a Sponsoring Organization

The interim outcomes noted above are beneficial for an organization where a PIP course is being given. And greater proficiency in reading, writing, speaking, and listening can be useful in all fields of academic study, as well as for communication and coordination in a business or industrial enterprise. The same holds true of the learning outcomes in interpersonal relationships which develop along with advances in intellectual skills.

Moving Toward Case-Mindedness

A mid-course 'Progress Review' can help participants to advance toward an all-important goal of every PIP course: *learning to take a case-minded approach to everyday experience.* What is said and decided, at each stock-taking meeting, provides evidence as to the stage currently reached by course members in developing their potential as productive workmates and farsighted managers. A few meetings are not, in themselves, sufficient to help course members progress far from where they started. Those who promptly begin to use what they learn can get ahead faster than those who do nothing (outside of class hours) with techniques and ideas which are new to them. Naturally, some people enter a course already far advanced in skills and attitudes which enable them to think and act in an everyday situation as though it were a human relations case, formally presented for

Outcomes

analysis and decision by group work. But whatever stage has been reached in the science and art of human relations, a significant advantage offered by a PIP course is that it facilitates a progressive shift of attention. Figure 5 indicates four typical stages during which the primary focus shifts from *a historical case* (presented to a study group for discussion and analysis) to *everyday situations* (in which the people who think, talk, and make decisions are actually involved).

In column 1, box 1, "THAT CASE" is capitalized to represent the idea that the center of interest, at least for most course members (in Stage 1), is on the case being discussed.

In column 1, box 2, PIP method is of less interest to most people, in Stage 1, than "THAT CASE," the case-for-the day. Nevertheless, sufficient attention is paid to PIP techniques so that observers can identify and report clear-cut evidences of technical advances in case analysis by course members.

In column 1, box 3, "this case" is scarcely noticed by most course members. Only outstanding participants can be expected immediately to recognize *the situation of the study group itself* as a 'case' which has much in common both with each historical case discussed and with the situations that students live through in everyday life.

In column 1, box 4, everyday situations are rarely recognized, at first, as 'cases' to which attitudes and skills of case method are applicable.

After this initial explanation, the few words in each of the other three columns in Figure 5 should be self-explanatory. But it may be useful to emphasize the progressive shift of focus by stages. Namely:

In column 2, (Stage 2) the primary focus of attention by course members is usually on "PIP METHOD." Many people quickly become interested in the varied and interactive techniques which they apply (with guidance from teachers) during class hours.

Figure 5

Progressive Shift of Focus Toward Case-Mindedness

STAGE 1	STAGE 2	STAGE 3	STAGE 4
"THAT CASE," a historical situation, of primary interest to students at the start of a course	"That Case," beginning to be subordinated to the application of method	"that case," the case-for-the-day recognized as a vehicle for PIP method	"that case," an everyday situation, viewed *case-mindedly*
PIP method, a five-step cycle of case analysis and other techniques, presented for experiment	METHOD coming into sharp focus as a technique to experiment with in class	(method), now so familiar as to be applied almost automatically	(method) taken for granted
"this case," the ongoing situation of the study group itself, scarcely noticed, at first, by most students	"this case," noticed sporadically, especially when writing or studying reports on group performance	"THIS CASE," center of attention beginning with the first *'progress review'* meeting	"This Case," observed and experimented in, as a sample of other situations (past and future) in which case method can be useful
(everyday situations outside of class) little relevance seen, at first, with what occurs during class hours	(everyday situations) some students begin to experiment with case method *outside of class hours*	Everyday Situations moving from the periphery toward the center of attention	EVERYDAY SITUATIONS becoming the center of attention and viewed as opportunities to integrate all aspects of case study

Column 3 represents the point (Stage 3) usually reached at the time of the first 'progress review.' Attention now centers on "THIS CASE," the ongoing situation of the study group itself. And, time permitting, outstanding students (some of whom may already hold managerial positions) can demonstrate their grasp of the concept that *'major issues' link historical cases, 'this case,' and many situations in everyday life.*

Column 4 (Stage 4) indicates a logical progression from that shown in column 3. At this fourth stage, learning begins to bear fruit in case-minded responses to everyday situations. These daily situations (in box 4, column 4) now constitute the main focus of attention. The other boxes in column 4 show how *case method, 'that (historical) case,'* and *'this case'* fall into place in relation to daily experience.

Favorable Long-Term Results for Individuals: Students and Teachers

Here are some oral reports from students made at final meetings. They may help to round out the picture of progress to be expected by the end of a PIP course. It should be borne in mind that, for each individual, the outcomes of any course are to some extent unique. But certain experiences and opinions have been reported so frequently that they may be regarded as typical.

- *From Subcommittees of Volunteer Discussion Leaders*
  - "Speaking before a group was a really instructive experience."
  - "Discussion of our case by the group gave us a composite view—what everyone saw in it. We were surprised to find how much more there was to be seen in a situation that we thought we knew inside-out."
  - "A discussion leader notices that the more minds take part in making a decision, the more ideas and

options become available. This could be particularly important when these other thinkers include people on whom final decision-makers must depend for results."
—"This job showed us hów important it is to create a climate where people feel able to speak freely; and we were in a position to draw out people who hadn't said much before."
—"Answering unexpected questions made us think on our feet."
—"The experience of being a discussion leader gives you practice in keeping your cool. You can use that in your everyday work."
—"All [four] of us have begun using this method in our regular jobs."
- *From Subcommittees of Observer-Reporters*
—"We had a chance to notice group dynamics, and when we visited around (during Step 4), we could see *how* people arrive at decisions."
—"When we compared our findings with earlier reports, we noticed that the same people have always tended to be in the same kind of opinion group: hard-nosed, or wanting to be 'nice to nice people'."
—"Putting your observations into a written report, especially when it is to be read by the people whose performance you are reporting on, is good mental discipline. You have to organize your findings and decide what to highlight and what to leave out. You have to watch your words."
—"Being an observer helps you learn how to listen, to absorb information, to interpret what people say. So you get a lot more out of the course after you've been an official observer."
- *From an Evaluators' Committee*

—"We all felt that as the course went on we were learning to become better analyzers, to think more objectively, and to make decisions that were more realistic."

—"Our chief recommendation is that the course should be longer, so everyone could take a turn in one (or better still in both) of the leading roles."

Long-Term Organizational Outcomes

Obviously, all favorable results, for students and teachers who are—or later become—organizational members are also beneficial for that organization. But a difficulty in reporting specific organizational outcomes consists in the circumstance that close and continued observation would be needed to get the facts. The Pigors team lacks staffing for systematic follow-up. However, a few indications of organizational outcomes have been given in the following ways:

Telephone calls or brief visits initiated by former students, now presidents of their own companies, or at the executive level in large organizations, have produced testimony that the PIP method was felt to have been useful. Here are two case examples:

• In one textile manufacturing company, PIP had been used for some years at managerial and supervisory levels. The labor relations director reported that what had been learned during these courses had enabled the organization drastically to reduce a previously large annual number of industrial disputes that went to arbitration. In the most recent year, all but three grievances had been settled at the supervisory level; and none had gone to arbitration.

• The president of a multi-plant manufacturing organization had attended one PIP session as part of an AMA course. Later that year, he arranged for a series of PIP meetings (to be given by the senior author as a consultant) at every level of management in the central plant. These courses proved so helpful that, subsequently, similar courses were given in decentralized plant locations. There, too, management representatives reported that PIP had contributed significantly to their development, and—indirectly—to improved labor relations.

Such reports, of which there have been many, provide convincing evidence that progress in this variant of orthodox case method can lead to practical outcomes. Differences between union officials and representatives of management can be settled promptly and satisfactorily (with minimum costs in time, money, and frustration) when parties to a given dispute have learned—

(1) to gather relevant information thoroughly, view it objectively, and report it accurately;
(2) to listen to one another with some degree of empathy as well as with close attention, intelligence, enlightened self-interest, and common sense;
(3) to recognize that the long-term goals which they share are more important than the short-term differences which temporarily divide them; and
(4) to develop "integrative solutions" in which all concerned get what they need most, by conceding some of what matters less—over the long-term.

For the future, perhaps the most significant outcomes of PIP will be owing to its qualities of self-renewal and spread. Since the 1950's, PIP has made its way into businesses and industries (often as continuing education units), government agencies, all branches of the armed services, and many colleges from coast to coast of the United States. During the 60's it spread to Mexico and overseas in Europe, India, and Japan. After initial courses, given by the senior author or by the Pigors team, other people (many of them training directors) took over the responsibility of keeping PIP going. Perhaps the most outstanding example of this development is the Kan Institute of Management Education in Tokyo. Mr.

Kan started as a student in a three-week course given by the Pigors in Tokyo and sponsored jointly by the State Department and the Committee for Economic Development in Japan. Soon afterward, Mr. Kan resigned his position as personnel administrator and for more than 15 years has made a full-time profession of organizing and leading PIP courses in Japan. Continuing correspondence has kept him in touch with new developments in the American PIP. But Mr. Kan has also made a few adaptations to meet special needs in Japan, and has developed Japanese cases to supplement the Pigors' material.

In mentioning this evidence that many people have found PIP useful, we make no claim that PIP is a panacea for all difficulties in industrial relations. What we do say is that this streamlined variant of orthodox case method has received wide recognition. When undertaken seriously, over a period of months or years, and with the classroom used as a social laboratory, for many people PIP has proved to be an effective way of learning how to interact productively with others.

Reference

Lee, I.J. *Customs and Crises in Communication: Cases for the Study of Some Barriers and Breakdowns.* New York: Harper and Brothers, Publishers, 1954; "The Case Method—A Point of View," pp. 1-42.

V.

RESOURCES

Fast, J., and B. Fast. *Talking Between the Lines: How We Mean More Than We Say.* New York: Viking, 1979.

Maier, N.R.F. *Principles of Human Relations: Applications to Management.* New York: John Wiley and Sons, Inc., 1952, pp. 62-86.

Pigors, P. Effective Communication in Industry: What Is Its Basis? The first Lt. Toland Memorial Fellowship Study to explore ways and means of improving employer-employee understanding and cooperation, National Association of Manufacturers of the United States of America, New York, 1949.

Pigors, P. Case Method, Chapter 35 in *Training and Development Handbook: A Guide to Human Resource Development,* sponsored by the American Society for Training and Development, Robert L. Craig, Editor. New York: McGraw-Hill Book Company, 1976.

Pigors, P., and C.A. Myers. *Personnel Administration: A Point of View and a Method.* New York: McGraw-Hill Book Company, 1977, eighth edition.

Pigors, P., and F. Pigors. Case Method on the Spot. *Adult Leadership,* December, 1954, Vol. 3, No. 6, pp. 7-8, 28-29. The first of two articles on the Incident Process.

Pigors, P., and F. Pigors. The Incident Process—Learning by Doing. *Adult Leadership,* January, 1955, Vol. 3, No. 7, pp. 5-7, 30.

Pigors, P., and F. Pigors. *The Incident Process: Case Studies for Management Development, Series I:* Practical Supervisory Problems, The Bureau of National Affairs, Inc., Washington D.C., 1955, 16 full-length Discussion Plans.

Pigors, P., and F. Pigors. *The Incident Process: Case Studies for Management Development, Series II:* Government Cases: Federal, State, and Local, BNA 1958, 13 full-length Discussion Plans.

Pigors, P., and F. Pigors. *The Incident Process: Case Studies for Management Development, Series III:* White Collar Cases: Office Supervision and Middle Management Cases, BNA 1965, 13 full-length Discussion Plans.

Pigors, P., and F. Pigors. *Case Method in Human Relations: The Incident Process,* New York: McGraw-Hill Book Company, 1961. Appendix 1: Abstracts of 11 full-length case reports.

Pigors, P., and F. Pigors. The Incident Process—A Method of Inquiry. *Nursing Outlook,* October, 1966, Vol. 14, No. 10, pp. 48-50.

Pigors, P., and F. Pigors. Operation Springboard for Management Development, Part I. *Personnel Journal,* April, 1967, Vol. 46, No. 4, pp. 214-218, 245; Part II, *Personnel Journal,* May, 1967, Vol. 46, No. 5, pp. 290-296.

Pigors, P., F. Pigors, and M. Tribou. *Professional Nursing Practice: Cases and Issues.* New York: McGraw-Hill Book Company, 1967.

Tribou, M. The Incident Process in Teaching. *Nursing Outlook,* January, 1965, Vol. 13, pp. 36-39.

Tribou, M. The Search before Research. In a senior seminar, students explore one of their own experiences, using the five phases of the search process to guide them through a systematic, independent inquiry—the forerunner of research. *Nursing Outlook,* October, 1966, Vol. 14, No. 10, pp. 51-53.

VI.

APPENDIX

The primary purpose of this Appendix is to provide materials needed to implement PIP's overall design in such a way as to achieve desirable results. A useful by-product may be a clearer understanding of PIP's concepts and terminology—including the related meanings of such terms as:
- "Incident,"
- case situation,
- case report, and
- Discussion Plan.

All items in this Appendix have proved their worth in helping teachers and students to interact productively; by making the most of existing circumstances and opportunities in each case study group. These learning-teaching tools and aids to development are:
1. Administrative and Social Preliminaries.
2. "Operation Springboard" (with instructions for use).
3. Proposed Goals for Participants in a PIP Course.
4. A Systematic Search Pattern for Fact-Finding.
5. Suggested Criteria for Selecting Observer-Reporters.
6. Selecting and Writing an "Incident."
7. Specifications for a Useful Case Report.
8. Sample Case Summary.
9. What's in a PIP Discussion Plan?
10. Sample Worksheet for Observer-Reporters.
11. Sample Fact-Finding Table (with suggestions for making one).
12. Interim Review Meeting—Proposed Goals and Agenda.
13. First Progress Review—Suggested Subcommittee Assignments.
14. Final Meeting—Proposed Goals and Agenda.

93

1. Administrative and Social Preliminaries

Before and during the first meeting of a PIP course, teachers need to meet the following responsibilities:

• *Enrollment,* such as to ensure a suitable number (between 12 and 25) and a useful mix of persons—all of whom know something as to: (1) what is expected of participants in the course, and (2) what they may hope to learn during the series of meetings.

• *Preparation of notebooks* for enrollees. Each notebook should contain a roster giving names and telephone numbers of participants. (In a business or industry, rosters should include job titles and departments.) These notebooks should be at each place before the start of the first meeting.

• *Preparation of other material* to be used at the first meeting: e.g., copies of *Operation Springboard* (item 2 in this Appendix); a *film* (if there will be time to use one); *tearsheets;* a *teacher's own notes and planning for group work* at this first meeting (including a flexible time schedule); copies of *proposed goals for participants during the course,* (all material for distribution should be on paper with holes that fit the notebooks); *tent cards* (with names printed in block letters on both sides so that everyone can see who all the others are); a *few blank cards* (in case of last-minute changes in enrollment); and two or three *heavy black markers* (so that course members can add numbers in one upper corner and perhaps nicknames in the other).

• *Arrangements* made for chairs, tables, ashtrays (unless there is an in-house rule against smoking); a *chalkboard* with chalk; or *overhead transparency projector.* Chairs should be set up in a horseshoe pattern, with adequate table space in front of each chair—for course members to take notes and spread out reference material; a *film projector* (if possible with an expert to operate it) should be in the conference room at least ten minutes before the meeting is scheduled to start. The 'first team' should also be on hand at least ten minutes early to check the projector; distribute notebooks; rearrange chairs (if they were left in rows after a lecture); and to call the cafeteria, if the coffee urn has not arrived before starting time. At this first meeting, it's a good investment to start by spending ten or 15 minutes over coffee. If a leisurely start is possible, a teacher (or team) can swap names and chat briefly with those who arrive early.

• When it's time to get down to business, *some direction can usefully be offered as to seating.* For reasons which will soon become apparent to participants, it is preferable that course members do *not sit next to persons whom they already know.* Nor should women and members of ethnic groups cluster together.

• If a quick check of the roster (as tent cards are put up) indicates that not everyone is present, any empty chairs should be on the

Appendix 95

discussion leader's extreme right, if numbering is to be done clockwise. These chairs, when occupied by late arrivals, will thus automatically receive the highest numbers. Numbering can be sequential, without leaving spaces between those who are present at the start of the first meeting.

- The time to explain and implement the *numbering procedure* (on tent cards) comes when all prompt arrivals are seated. It is advisable to mention that using numbers instead of names will save time throughout the course for observer-reporters. When participants number their own cards according to the seating arrangement, no one can suppose that the numbers represent any kind of merit-rating system.
- *Mutual introductions* come next. A natural start is with self-introduction by the discussion leader (and introduction of the first observer-reporter, if any). Use of first names for leaders helps to set the informal tone that characterizes PIP. (Tent cards for teachers or teams naturally include last names also, just as all the other cards do.) A brief explanation of the observer-reporter's role is also useful at the start. Otherwise, course members may wonder: "Why all this writing?" When this role description can be outlined (in two or three minutes) *by* the observer-reporter, more can be communicated than could be conveyed by anyone else. As course members introduce themselves, *everyone can check the roster.* Does some last-minute change in enrollment (or perhaps a recent transfer or promotion) call for any correction?
- *Operation Springboard* makes an excellent start for the actual business of the opening meeting. (A copy of Op.S. is given as item 2 in this Appendix.)
- Then, if the meeting can be at least two hours long, a *film* can usefully be shown—subdivided into several sequences, with opportunities for course members to make, discuss, and test their predictions as to what various characters in the film will do next.
- *Specific orientation to course objectives* can be provided by distributing and briefly discussing *proposed goals for the course.* (See item 3.)
- *Technical induction* can be set in motion as *PIP's five-step analytical cycle* is outlined (perhaps using prepared tearsheets.) If desired, copies of that outline can be distributed, along with samples of a case summary and a Step 3 diagram. (A sample case summary is given as item 8 in this Appendix, and a Step 3 diagram, with key, was given in Chapter III.)

The above design of a first meeting, over the years, has given course members a head start on the analytical work which begins with the second meeting of the new PIP.

2. "Operation Springboard"

This exercise has proved valuable when used toward the start of the first meeting in a PIP course. It serves (1) to bring out assumptions and attitudes that influence behavior in human relations, and (2) to demonstrate—from the outset—the advantages of having students discuss their opinions, including their differences, *with one another*— instead of merely exchanging questions and answers with a teacher.

Instructions for Students

Please put your name (and organizational position, if any) on the attached survey sheet. Then read the statements, one at a time, indicating your immediate reaction as follows:

1. If you *A*gree with the statement as written, put an "X" in the box marked "A."
2. If you *Dis*Agree with the statement as written, put an "X" in the box marked "DA." (If time permits, *underline* words with which you strongly disagree.)
3. If you feel doubtful about any printed statement, put an "X" in the box which corresponds *more nearly* to your opinion and *circle that box.* (If time permits, edit the statement to make it clearer or more acceptable to you, but without changing the record of your first reaction.)
4. If you AGREE with one part of a statement and DISAGREE with another, put an "X" in each box and mark the start of each part either "A" or "DA."
5. Before handing in the completed form, please tear off this instruction sheet.

Thank you.

Operation Springboard: Opinion Survey

Please Print
Name .... Position ....

1. The chief responsibility of managers in regard to administrative communication is to state their meaning clearly .... | A | DA |
2. Inner motivation is more powerful than external incentives .... | A | DA |
3. Members of every work group should have opportunities to make suggestions about organizational decisions whose outcome will affect them .... | A | DA |
4. What employees do off company property and on their own time is of no concern to management .... | A | DA |
5. Women should not be promoted to managerial

(Continued on Page 97)

positions. They are not up to the job. Men don't like working under women .... A | DA
6. From the viewpoint of authority, there is no longer any important difference between line and staff positions .... A | DA
7. People will work harder and faster if they always have a little more work ahead of them than they can possibly do .... A | DA
8. An employer has a right to expect that employees will subordinate their personal goals to organization-wide objectives .... A | DA
9. Managers must make administrative decisions, but should not be expected to explain their reasons (to subordinates) .... A | DA
10. To compensate for past discrimination, women and members of minority groups should be recruited for jobs, at every organizational level, in numbers that match their proportions in the total (national) population .... A | DA

3. Proposed Goals for Participants in a PIP Course

In the Pigors' view, the dual overall goal is (1) sizing up real-life situations, and (2) interacting productively with colleagues. During this series of meetings, there will be opportunities to apply many of the ideas that will be recognized as relevant for "people in cases."

Acquiring experience *at the level of changing* isn't easy. It entails modifying habits of thinking, talking, listening, interpreting, and—in other ways—responding productively to events and people. Making such changes is a lifelong assignment. But anyone can make significant headway, even within a few months, by working steadily toward the following sub-goals:

1. Becoming more aware of, and perhaps reassessing—
- *one's own assumptions, attitudes, and preconceptions* about other people and about work. (These subjective forces inevitably affect what anyone can see, say, decide, and do.)
- *the way in which one arrives at important decisions.* (For example, do you often jump to conclusions, on the basis of scanty and unverified information? Or do you habitually keep an open mind until you have established facts, clarified issues for action, and given due weight to the opinions of other people?)
- one's current proficiency in *applying a kind of understanding* which blends intellectual capacity, appreciative ability, and common sense.

- *possibilities and prerequisites for friendly and reasonable communication* in a psychological climate that fosters mutual understanding and a free exchange of ideas.
2. *Refining skills of situational diagnosis (case analysis) and productive interaction.* For example:
    - Repeatedly searching for underlying meanings of small-scale incidents, by
    —getting facts needed to visualize an incident in the context of its total situation.
    —summarizing, analyzing, and weighing these facts before:
    - making short-term decisions that will stand the test of time;
    - linking such decisions, in one's mind, with long-term corporate goals;
    - developing a capacity for two complementary kinds of decision-making: (1) forming independent opinions; and (2) contributing to group decisions;
    - helping to build a consensus which represents the best thinking of persons who began by differing from one another;
    - habitually taking an experimental and experiential approach to new ideas and current events; and
    - acquiring the knack of shifting one's focus back and forth between *those cases* (the historical situations which will be discussed); *this case* (the ongoing situation of the study group itself); and *everyday situations* (lived through outside of class hours). When this shift of focus has become habitual, a student will have developed *a case-minded way of looking at, and living through, current events.*

As course members exercise such skills and work toward the sub-goals mentioned above, they can't fail to develop their managerial and executive potential.

4. A Systematic Search Pattern for Fact-Finding

This pattern is based on the hypothesis that the following interrelated variables are always worth looking into.
1. *Technical features*: e.g., work methods; mechanical or electronic equipment; and formal organizational relationships.
2. *The Human Element*: e.g., individual personalities—each with its unique pattern of inner motivation, special capabilities, and weaknesses; informal social relationships.
3. *Space/Time Coordinates*: e.g., the Where, When, Sequence, Duration, and Pace of current events; the natural tempo of individuals (in relation to that imposed by work requirements, and presented by those with whom they continually interact).
4. *Environmental Conditions*: e.g., temperature, humidity, ventilation, lighting, cleanliness, and orderliness of the work place.

Appendix

5. *A Policy Framework*: e.g., an overall, consistent, yet flexible system of guidelines for making administrative decisions and taking action.

A leader who can interest members of a study group in trying out some such systematic search pattern is giving them a tool which will also be useful in their everyday work relationships.

5. Suggested Criteria for Selecting Observer-Reporters

They should (if possible) be course members:
(1) with demonstrated interest and ability in:
  —analyzing cases,
  —thinking objectively,
  —listening empathically,
  —taking legible and adequate notes (not necessarily in shorthand),
  —reaching reasonable decisions,
  —making practical recommendations, and
  —communicating clearly and acceptably;
(2) who have time to do some work for the course *outside of scheduled conference hours* (possibly a total of ten or more hours during a period of a week or so before and after the team's case is presented);
(3) with whom the team leader feels psychologically comfortable and also, preferably, can work conveniently; and
(4) who have *not* previously served as observer-reporters.

When the above specifications can be met by any participant who has previously been a rather silent course member, the opportunity to play an important role in group work may be especially beneficial for that individual.

6. Selecting and Writing an "Incident"

Selection. Every real-life situation, and therefore every comprehensive case report, contains a succession of incidents, e.g., major or minor climaxes. At each of them, action decisions need to be made. But to trigger off fact-finding questions by case students, *the* Incident should be selected from somewhere near the middle of a case report. Then, it will be possible for the discussion leader to provide (in Step 2) information as to how the Incident built up; and (in Step 5) what actually was decided and done right afterwards, and what happened in the immediate sequel.

Earmarks of an effective "Incident."
- It is a short sketch (about half a page) of an actual event.
- The end of the Incident is written in the present tense (to indicate that the time for coping with the difficulty is "now").
- At first glance, the events and issues pictured may seem trivial.

- Beneath the surface, discerning readers can glimpse major issues. (For example, is there a challenge to authority, or some difficulty arising in part from organizational structure, regular practice, or corporate policy?)
- Two or more persons (or parties to a dispute) are depicted as being at odds with one another.
- It is evident that at least one of them is taking immediate issues seriously (seeing them either as "straws in the wind" or as "the last straw").
- This brief sketch is *vivid*, with *touches of drama* (such as can be given by quoting direct dialogue among persons who are stirred up). To meet this specification, it is permissible to word indirect discourse as direct *quotations.*
- There is room for difference, among reasonable people, in deciding how best to cope with the Incident.

7. Specifications for a Useful Case Report

1. *Selection.* The case situation should highlight *live issues* (though the events which illustrate them need not necessarily have occurred recently). The case should also give promise of arousing *lively interest* in members of a given study group.

Thus, even in selecting, and still more in writing, a case report, a discussion leader needs to think simultaneously about two case situations, *that case* (the one which is to be presented) and *this case* (the current situation of the study group itself). This bifocal view shows up in—

2. *A written case report* containing:
    - a well-selected and effectively written *Incident* (which meets criteria outlined in item 6 of this Appendix);
    - *adequate coverage of information* about the case as a whole, e.g., relevant information on the *technical feature*; the *human element* (possibly with a few inferences based on clear-cut evidence as to what people have said and done); *space/time coordinates* (the where, when, duration, and sequence of events); *policy framework* (as shown by an organization chart, a contract provision, or a corporate policy); and significant *environmental conditions* (weather, time of day, season of the year, working conditions).
    - *documentation of information offered as factual*;
    - *identification of any inferences* written into the case report along with mention of the basis for each; and
    - *objectively worded statements* (insofar as possible, though especially in a summary, subjective judgments almost inevitably creep in).

Appendix 101

In the subsection on the human element, an exception to the coverage rule should be made in regard to the *personality of the individual* whose role is to be taken (collectively) by case students. Experience shows that providing such information encourages second-guessing as to *what that person would do,* instead of developing an independent opinion as to what *anyone in that organizational role could most appropriately do.*

In reporting a case that went to arbitration, and when a hearing has been held, additional items of information should include *positions taken and evidence presented by the contending parties.* (That material is usually fraught with feeling. Nevertheless, *it is a fact* that the statements were made. An impartial arbitrator is obligated to take account of them in the written opinion that goes with the Award.)

8. Sample Case Summary (Relating to "Staff/Line Communication Blocks")

Recently, Section B (General Agency Contracts Division) has been swamped with extra work because of a change in policy options. Mr. Bombara requested action to lighten the overload. Mr. March decided that conversion to machine operations was the answer.

Last week, a Special Project Unit was set up across the hall from Mr. Bombara's Division, with Mr. March in charge. (Staff experts under him include Ms. Harris as supervisor.) Mr. March requested from Mr. Bombara "three good, dependable girls."

Betty was one of the clerks who was temporarily reassigned. Betty (not quite 19) was hired as a clerk, Job Grade 2, 11 months ago, immediately after graduating from high school. She started in Section A as a trainee for "Junior Change Clerk." Because Betty has near-point vision, her application form carries the note: "Close figure work—limitation." But Mr. Baker has been assured that her myopia should not be regarded as a handicap for general office work.

Betty soon showed herself to be intelligent, accurate, reliable, and easy to get along with. Her first performance appraisal was "good" in all respects, with perfect attendance. After her six-month probationary period, she was upgraded to "Junior Change Clerk."

Three months ago, Betty began training for the position of Change Clerk in Section B. She was pleased, because at the end of that training period (usually about a year), she could expect to move up to Job Grade 3. Also, she likes this more varied work.

On Wednesday of last week, Betty and two other clerks in Mr. Bombara's Division were told that they were being temporarily reassigned to the Special Project Unit. Betty expressed reluctance to interrupt her training. However, she acquiesced when assured that this temporary reassignment would not interfere with her anticipated promotion. (At the time of the Incident, neither Bombara nor Baker knows how long the Special Project will continue.)

That same morning, Betty and the other clerks started work in the Special Project Unit. (It was the first week of operations there.) During the first coffee break, Betty rushed back and appealed to supervisor Walker. Bursting into tears, she insisted that the pressure and confusion in the Special Project Unit were unbearable. She urgently requested permission to resume her training in Section B. Mr. Walker calmed her down, and she returned to the Special Project Unit.

This afternoon (four working days after her temporary reassignment), Mr. Bombara received a call from Mr. March demanding an immediate replacement for Miss Brown (Betty), who is "impossible . . . [because] she can't do *anything* right."

Mr. Bombara is much surprised and greatly upset. He immediately called for "me" (his Assistant Manager). "I" (Mr. Baker) also expressed surprise that a person like Betty has been making so many mistakes. Mr. Bombara then recalled Betty's reluctance to accept this reassignment and apparently surmised that she has deliberately been doing poor work in order to get sent back to Section B.

As Assistant Manager, "I" normally have little contact with clerks. But I have complete confidence in our supervisors (Coit and Walker) who keep in close touch with all clerks in the Division. I also have a friendly relationship with Mr. Bombara, whose administrative abilities I greatly respect. I agree with him that we can't tolerate direct action by clerks (such as he suspects that Betty has taken). The incident ended when he told me to "take care of it." I feel sure that he will support me in any reasonable decision.

It is now 3:30 p.m. and Betty's replacement is expected to start work tomorrow morning.

9. What's in a PIP Discussion Plan?

In a thorough Discussion Plan for group work by PIP, the following three common elements show up in each of the five parts (sections): (1) *a case report;* (2) *a Plan maker's analysis and short-term decisions* relating to that case; and (3) *flexible preparations* for productive interaction while that case is being discussed. These elements fit into a Plan, or are appended to it, as follows:

1. *A case report,* beginning in Part I, features the *Incident.* Most of the information on the case situation is contained in Part II (written out as resource material for a discussion leader). Some of this information may be prepared as separate *Attachments* (for distribution to course members) and merely cued into Part II by title. Part V provides the final bits of information on the case: what happened right after the Incident.

Appendix

2. *Analysis and short-term decisions relating to 'that case' appear as follows:*
   - in Part I, as choice and wording of the Incident;
   - in Part II, as selection and wording of factual information (possibly also a few inferences with the basis for them);
   - in Part III, as a Plan maker's independent diagram of interactive factors, with a key specifying sub-issues, and as a formulation of what the Plan maker sees as the immediate issue posed by the Incident;
   - in Part IV, the main text begins with a list of options—all of them (supposedly) feasible alternatives for short-term decisions. A Special Attachment (normally not distributed to the group-at-large) contains the Plan maker's short-term decision and reasoning—either for administrative action, or in the form of an impartial arbitrator's Award and "Opinion" (written reasoning); and
   - in Part V, the main text should include a Step-5 diagram showing a Plan maker's view of major issues in the case situation as a whole, and some of their interrelationships. An opinion as to their relative importance is indicated by the numbering of these diagrammed issues.

Appended to Part V, a Special Attachment gives a Plan maker's answers to the usual Step-5 questions. When the leader is a student, this Attachment, and the Special Attachment for Part IV, should be turned in to the teacher. Both documents offer significant evidence as to ability in case analysis.

Not all of the above-mentioned material can realistically be viewed as separate from some items which can also be classified as belonging to the third component of a PIP Plan.

3. *Flexible preparation for group work.* This element appears as:
   - A detailed but *flexible timetable* for all suboperations which may possibly be performed, to be implemented by a timekeeper (to keep group work on schedule).
   - Nature and tone of the *Suggestion* for getting into the case as a whole. When perceptively written, with members of a given study group in mind, this invitation to "come on in and take responsibility for coping with an incident," can be such that these individuals certainly could, and probably will, accept it as a challenging assignment.

These three elements also appear in each section as follows:

In Part I, timing of the Incident (within the total timespan of the case situation as reported) and wording of the Incident can serve as a launching pad for questions by course members as they explore the circumstances surrounding the incident.

In Part II, arrangement of topical subheadings can make it easy and quick to doublecheck or amplify some answer already given; careful preparation (as Attachments for distribution) of all materials that course members will need for close study and future reference; cueing in titles of these Attachments at appropriate places; arranging separate piles for each Attachment; and self-reminders, such as anticipated timing of fact-finding and for distributing a written summary (perhaps to supplement a sketchy oral summary from the study group).

In Part III, preparation for group work may appear, *in writing*, solely as a self-reminder; such as: "Don't 'tell 'em.' Ask them."

In Part IV, planning shows up as notes on whether role-playing, presentations by spokespersons, or both, seem likely to appeal to course members as the most effective way to present subcommittee opinions. If there *may* be role-playing, what arrangements need to be made to keep each skit within five minutes or so? If group members opt for both forms of presentation, what should the sequence be? Further planning, written into Part IV, may consist of notes on available techniques of group dynamics that might be useful.

Example of Standard Outline

An appropriate design for such a three-component, five-part Discussion Plan is indicated by the following standard outline (with sample self-reminders).

Part I: Studying the Incident. Self-reminders: Distribute copies of the Incident and of a partial organization chart pertaining to the case situation. Allow three or four minutes for study. (Sample "Suggestions" were appended to Incidents given in Chapter II.)

But when an Incident calls for an Arbitrator's Award, the following form may be used:

"Try to imagine yourself in the position of an impartial arbitrator. This dispute has been referred to you after the parties failed to settle it during the regular grievance procedure.

"If you actually *were* an impartial arbitrator, you would hold a hearing, listen to conflicting (partisan) testimony; ask questions; and establish as many indisputable facts as possible. Then, (in view of relevant provisions in the labor agreement) you would study and weigh documentary evidence. Finally, you would render an Award and outline your reasoning—in writing.

" 'Today' you can get verified facts from the discussion leader. And you will not be expected to work out a reasoned opinion by yourself, or to write out your reasoning. However,—during Step 4—you will be expected to form and express an opinion of your own. In doing so, your aim should be to approximate the thoroughness and objectivity that befit an impartial arbitrator."

Part II: Providing Information on the Case as a Whole—up to the end of the Incident. Self-reminders: In general, supply information *only* in answer to a question which specifically asks for it. *Do not*, at this stage, *supply any information* as to what happened *after* the Incident.

The usual subheadings in Part II are:
(a) *Place* and *time* of the Incident, and *total timespan of the case.*
(b) *Names of persons* directly and indirectly involved in the Incident.
(c) *Build-up of the Incident* (events and behaviors).
(d) *Notes on people listed above* (biographical data, informal relationships, personality traits, employment record, etc.).
(e) *Organizational notes* which: (1) amplify and explain the organization chart, and, if necessary, (2) include information on standard practice, relevant sections of the labor agreement, plant rules, and corporate policy. (Some of this material may require careful study and is, therefore, provided in the form of *attachments* that are cued into the main text.)
(f) *Relevant technical data:* e.g., work methods and equipment; composition of work teams, etc.

In a case which is 'now' at the stage of arbitration, contentions of the disputing parties can be outlined in a special *attachment.*

Part III: Determining What Is Immediately at Stake—at the time of the Incident. Self-reminders:
(a) act as recording secretary while students offer ideas for a Step 3 diagram;
(b) if group work is seriously inadequate, be prepared to ask a few leading questions; and
(c) help group members to *formulate,* and *agree upon,* a suitable statement of the immediate Issue.

Part IV: Making Group Decisions: On the Issue and to Clarify Reasoning. Self-reminders: Lead group members through as many of the following suboperations as time permits:
(a) *Selecting options for short-term decisions.* Perhaps some alternatives will be added to the prepared list.
(b) *Conferring in opinion groups.* Make sure that each subcommittee elects a chairperson, as the first order of business. Any need to urge emphasis on *reasons* which support decisions? Allow about 20 minutes for work in these small-group conferences.
(c) *Presenting*—to the group-at-large—*the various committee opinions.* Help course members to recognize due time limits—especially for role-playing. Discourage arguing.

(d) (if time permits) *Comparing and appraising opinions and presentations.*

Part V: *What Can We Learn From the Case?* Self-reminders:
(a) If necessary, remind course members not to revert to arguments about short-term decisions. Instead, urge them to focus on *needs, opportunities, and difficulties* which relate to long-term action on major issues in the case as a whole—as indicated by answers to Step-5 questions.
(b) Possibly offer suggestions as to the composition of subgroups. Schedule *at least 20 minutes* for this kind of conferring.
(c) As spokespersons report subgroup answers, *write identifying words* in three columns on the chalkboard (or overhead transparency). If more than one subcommittee has considered any one question, solicit reports on one question at a time.. Suggest that spokespersons, *after the first,* mention only those portions of their reports *which differ* from what was said by a previous speaker. (Relevant new material consists of additions, deletions, or significant differences in wording.)
(d) When it is time *to correlate* items among the three columns of answers to the Step-5 questions, try to do no more than draw connecting lines which indicate student thinking.
(e) Provide the *historical* (short-term) *decision,* and any other information available as to what happened after the Incident.
(f) (If time permits) Solicit from students ideas for a *diagram of major issues* in the case situation as a whole. Will there be any opportunity to help students recognize that some of these recurrent issues are typical of most situations in which people work together for results?

Appendix

10. Sample Worksheet for Observer-Reporters

TITLE OF CASE: .... DATE OF MEETING ....

TIME:

QUESTION NUMBER	MEMBER NUMBER		TOPICS
Q: 1	M:		
Q: 2	M:		
Q: 3	M:		
Q: 4	M:		
Q: 5	M:		
Q: 6	M:		
Q: 7	M:		
Q: 8	M:		
Q: 9	M:		
Q: 10	M:		

(Prepare in sets numbered 1-10, 11-20, 21-30, etc.)

11. Sample Fact-Finding Table

(This table pictures questioning on the case: "Staff/Line Communication Blocks.")

Date .... Place .... Number in the series ...., Case title ....

Topics   Questions in sequence asked*

	1-10	11-20	21-30	31-37	TOTALS
A. Betty–Motivation; family; record (work and conduct)	4:26 5:1 8:3 10:3	12:29 13:2 14:15 20:21	26:12		9
B. Other clerks from our division	7:5	16:16 17:16 18:16 19:16		34:?	6
C. Management communication–to Betty; Baker; Bombara	9:3	11:29	23:20 24:21 25:10 29:21		6
D. Organization	1:3 2:3 3:3 6:5		28:17		5
E. Management relationships: Bombara-Baker; Bombara-Harris; Bombara and Baker-Harris				33:1 35:26 36:12	3
F. The Special Project: Betty's work assignment		15:7	22:21		2
G. Baker: His information re. Special Project and Clerks			21:21	37:21	2
H. Harris: Ability as a supervisor			27:12	32:17	2
I. March: What he knows about Betty; previous managerial experience			30:3	31:21	2

Grand Total: 37

*In each pair of figures, the lefthand number shows the sequence of the question. The righthand number indicates who asked the question.

Appendix

Suggestions for Making a Fact-Finding Table
1. *Preparing.* In the lefthand margin of the worksheets, classify each question by topic: e.g., "relationships" (formal and informal), "technical," "space/time," "personal."
After figuring subtotals for each topic, set up an alphabetical sequence of topics which indicates the amount of interest shown by the group as a whole.
2. *Tabulating.* In the lefthand column, indicate alphabetical sequence of topics. Next, enter double-digit symbols (1) showing the sequence of questions, and (2) identifying questioners.
3. *Checking and completing.* Before entering topic totals in the extreme righthand column, verify that the subtotals match the numbers recorded in each (horizontal) set of topic-boxes. If they do not match, run your eye down the vertical columns. Are there ten questions in each column? If not, go back to your worksheets.
Finally, do the topic totals add up to the grand total (recorded on worksheets)? If not, is it because a few questions were asked in Steps 3 or 4?
If the time spent on asking fact-finding questions is to be reported, subtract from the total elapsed time for Step 2 the time spent in *summarizing.* Also, if questions about facts were asked in Steps 3 or 4, that amount of time should be included.

12. Interim Review Meeting—Proposed Goals and Agenda
The *chief goals* for this meeting may be stated as:
- To sum up and appraise accomplishments and progress to date.
- To plan and discuss possible changes in practice.
- To reach consensus as to which of these proposals are to be implemented.

Proposed agenda. The most important items will be the following:
- *Conferring in small groups;* each subcommittee focusing on one or more of the basic variables in *this case* (the situation of the work group itself). Specific suggestions as to topics and subtopics will be offered to each subcommittee. To establish and evaluate facts, a combined Step-2 and Step-5 approach is recommended for all subcommittees, ending with the usual Step-5 questions. Consistent procedure will make it convenient to compare and correlate the various committee reports.
- *Explanations* will be given by the teacher if any of these reports reveal misunderstandings about PIP's technical method or current features.
- *Proposals for changes* may call for further explanations. For example, it often happens that some proposed change has been tried in a previous course and found to be impractical. Other suggestions

for change might go beyond the general guidelines that represent PIP's policy framework.
- *Reaching consensus on proposed changes* will probably have to be the last item on the agenda. For the convenience of volunteer discussion leaders and observer-reporters who wish to implement agreed-upon plans, group decisions will be duly noted in the official report on this crucial meeting.

13. First Progress Review–
Suggested Subcommittee Assignments

Before appraising our work together so far, we need to establish facts about basic variables in our work situation. Consider such topics as:

1. *Technical features:* PIP as a work method. What does the record show, and what is your appraisal, with regard to—
   - relevance to daily work of technical skills exercised;
   - group progress in some or all of these skills;
   - caliber of instruction and of written reports;
   - usefulness of group dynamics (including all small-group work); and
   - course structure, to date, and plans for leadership by students?
2. *Human element,* for example:
   - size of the study group; range of departments represented; proportions of male/female; white/ethnic; staff/line;
   - style of managing demonstrated by the instructor;
   - evidences of effective teamwork; with teaching partner? With students?
   - psychological climate of meetings; and
   - informal relationships among participants. (For example, how soon did all participants know each other by name? How many leading teams have already signed up? Opportunities for friendly consultation by student leaders with members of the 'first team'?)
3. *Space/time coordinates* (working conditions), for example:
   - Convenient location of conference room? Suitable seating arrangements? Ample space for small-group work?
   - Timing of meetings: time of day; day of week; length of each meeting and of the whole course; time spent in each step of the analytical cycle; timing for issuing written reports.

14. Final Meeting–Proposed Goals and Agenda
Goals

To achieve the same goals as those for a productive *interim review,* a slightly different agenda is suggested for this *summary meeting.*

Appendix

Proposed Agenda

1. A useful beginning can be made by spending a few minutes in an experiment whose value would be nullified by advance explanation.

2. The second item of business should, as before, be subcommittee conferences. This time, the composition of small groups, and the topics to be discussed, can be different from what they could have been at mid-course. Now, volunteer discussion leaders and observer-reporters can get together (each in their own subgroup) to consider such questions as:

- What benefits, if any, have we derived from the *extra work* we did as leaders?
- What changes, if any, would we recommend—for future PIP courses—in role descriptions, role performance, or other aspects of this work situation? (Members of these two subcommittees may wish also to consider the questions proposed for discussion in the third subgroup, or other matters which seem to them important.)

A third subcommittee (of "evaluators-at-large") might emphasize two points:

- *changes that have occurred* since the mid-course review meeting (which decisions for making changes were implemented? How well did these innovations work out?); and
- *long-term goals* agreed upon. (To what extent have these goals been achieved? What recommendations might be made for changes in future PIP courses?)

3. *Reports* from spokespersons and discussion of findings would naturally come next. Then there might be a *brief report from the teacher* on results of the first item on the agenda.

4. Finally, there may be time to identify *major issues* that have appeared in several cases which have been analyzed. These issues should be explicitly related both to goals agreed upon for this course and to objectives in everyday work situations of participants.

PAUL PIGORS is Professor Emeritus, Industrial Relations, at the Massachusetts Institute of Technology. He received his B.S. Cum Laude degree from Harvard College in 1924 and the M.A. and Ph.D. degrees from Harvard University in 1925 and 1927, respectively. Dr. Pigors has been a Consultant to the U.S. Army Management Training Agency; a Panel Member of the American Arbitration Association; Charter Member, National Academy of Arbitrators; and an impartial arbitrator listed by the Federal Mediation and Conciliation Service. He has been a lecturer and discussion group leader at courses and conferences conducted throughout the world.

FAITH PIGORS was educated at Milton Academy, Milton, Massachusetts, the Ecole Normale de Musique in Paris, and Radcliffe College. She has been a case writer and editorial consultant in case writing and, with Paul Pigors, member of a husband-wife teaching team. She has conducted PIP sessions in such countries as England, Mexico, and Japan, in addition to work in the United States, with the longest consecutive teaching appointment being with the John Hancock Mutual Life Insurance Company, Boston, from 1958 to 1973.